QUEEN OF DARKNESS

Book Twelve of the Hayle Coven Novels

PATTI LARSEN

Copyright © 2012 Patti Larsen
All rights reserved.
Cover art © by Valerie Bellamy. All rights reserved.
dog-earbookdesign.com
Edited by Annetta Ribken, freelance Goddess.
wordwebbing.com
ISBN: 978-1-988700-20-5

All rights reserved. This book or any portion thereof may not be reproduced or used in any manner whatsoever without the express written permission of the author or publisher except for the use of brief quotations in critical articles or reviews.

This is a work of fiction. Names, places, businesses, characters and incidents are either the product of the author's imagination or are used in a fictitious manner. Any resemblance to actual persons, living or dead, actual events or locales is purely coincidental.

Find out more about Patti Larsen at **pattilarsen.com**

ALSO BY
PATTI LARSEN

The Hayle Coven Universe

The Hunted Series
Fiona Fleming Cozy Mysteries
The Nightshade Cases
The Clone Chronicles
The Diamond City Trilogy
Didi and the Gunslinger

and much, much more.
Find your new favorite author at
pattilarsen.com
Sign up for new releases
bit.ly/pattilarsenemail

Chapter One

The giant wave crashed over my head about a second after I turned to see it coming. Blue water closed around me. The fading sun shone through, dispersing as I went deeper, shoved down to thud against the sandy bottom as inertia took over. My lungs spasmed, body begging for air I hadn't had time to draw before going under. The brightly-painted surfboard rocketed to the surface without me, tether line jerking on my ankle. My body tried to figure out which way was up while the foaming rush of water drove me down and rolled me forward, headfirst into the gritty bottom.

I suppose I should have panicked, considering. Anyone else would have, I'm sure of it. But even in that moment of mortal terror, my logical mind shrugged.

Immortality had its benefits.

My demon wasn't quite so calm about the whole

thing. She started to shriek the moment we went under, clawing for freedom while Shaylee screamed at me in counterpoint. I barely had time to catch myself as I began to flip butt over end before my demon shredded the edge of the veil and threw us all into it.

Sometimes sharing my body with three other consciousnesses was a bit of a pain in the ass.

I hit the dry beach hard as my demon dropped us free only feet from the surf, coughing up the bit of water I'd managed to inhale. The sound of screaming, yeah, I was familiar with screaming, headed my way, my name being called in panic.

Strong hands grasped me and flipped me over. A pair of arctic blue eyes fading from human to wolf staring into mine told me I was in a world of trouble. Charlotte growled softly under her breath, my ever-faithful bodywere recovering from yet another freak out I caused her.

Hardly my fault. Surfing had been Sashenka's idea.

My college roommate and best friend fell to her knees beside me, concern clear on her face as she reached for me around Charlotte, even when the weregirl snapped at Sashenka with her teeth as a warning to stay back. I pushed Charlotte aside and sat up, spluttering out a mouthful of sand, looking down in disgust. What a mess.

"I'm fine," I said.

Seriously, how embarrassing. Sashenka's surfer friends

had come to crowd around and check on me too. And while I really wasn't interested in any of the guys, my love life about as complicated as I was willing to have it, it still kicked my ego hard in the soft place knowing how much of an idiot I'd made of myself.

No more surfing. My demon chuffed her full agreement.

The gang backed off with cheery comments: "Great ride, Sydilicious!", "Watch those big ones, Syderino!", before running off to leap once more into the brink of yet another gigantic wave.

I tried all week to learn to surf, and though I'd even thrown in a little water magic as a cheat, I just had to admit there wasn't an athletic bone in my body. Outside soccer. And I'd given it up years ago.

Sashenka stayed with me, her hand lifting the severed tether, surfboard nowhere to be seen. "Tallah's going to kill you," she grinned. "That was her favorite board."

I grinned back, wiping at the abrasive sand covering most of my body. "Good thing I'm immortal then, huh?"

Charlotte was not taking this well. "That's no excuse to pull a stupid stunt," she snarled. Her accent was stronger than normal, a sure sign she was losing her temper.

"I didn't purposely try to drown, Charlotte," I said. "The wave just took me by surprise."

Her eyes narrowed, the wolf in them restless and full

of anxiety. "You might be immortal, but if you are hurt doing something like this again, I'll kill you myself." She stood and stalked off, grumbling and muttering to herself in her native language. Had to be swearwords.

Had to be.

I sent Sashenka off to keep surfing, taking a quick dip to clean off the sand before lying back in the dying daylight to watch the others ride the waves. I wasn't sure why, but as I did I thought of Trill and Owen. The Zornovs had been gone about two months with no word from them. I knew they had their own destinies to deal with, and Trill was hopefully busy building a maji army now we knew the Brotherhood was planning a world and plane-wide takeover. I still worried about them.

All alone.

There was a time when family didn't mean much to me, my desire to get out of the witch lifestyle and leave it all behind the driving force in my life. But since I'd regained control and taken over half-leadership of the coven, family meant more to me than I expected. And now I knew I was immortal, thanks to my demon blood, the Sidhe princess and vampire essence living inside me, being part of something bigger was even more important.

I didn't even want to think about what Trill said, how I was evolving into maji—not just one of the blood line, but an actual maji like the meddling Iepa—nor consider what being a creator would mean. Hard enough knowing

I'd outlive every person I loved. Well, almost. I had a few undead and demon family members who shared my longevity. And yet, I couldn't help but worry about them, too.

They were long lived, yes. But I was immortal. Never grow old, never die.

Ever.

Shudder.

Made me want to curl up under the covers sometimes and hide from the world. Or hug my family so close to me they'd never be free. The truth was so big, the reality of it so overwhelming. I just couldn't deal.

So I shoved it down, smothered it in a healthy dose of denial and pretended nothing changed even though I knew everything had.

Besides, most people would kill to have what I did. And here I was, complaining? Maybe if being immortal came with a quiet, peaceful lifestyle, I'd be less anxious. But mine tended to the "nothing, nothing, nothing, save the world before it explodes, nothing" variety.

Sashenka and Charlotte finally returned, the Hensley second carrying her board, my bodywere lugging the one I'd lost in the surf.

"Saved by the werewolf," Sashenka grinned, bumping shoulders with Charlotte who looked startled at the contact. "Tallah will forgive you now."

I climbed to my feet, grinning at the weregirl. Not

very often did someone catch her off guard. "Thanks for saving me," I said with a perfectly straight face.

Sashenka had to go and ruin it by giggling.

Charlotte shoved the board into my arms and snarled, stalking up the beach to the house, body tense, her motions jerky and abrupt, a far cry from her normal flowing walk.

"I didn't mean to make her angry." Sashenka and her empathy. I winked and hefted the board, following Charlotte's path with my best friend beside me.

"Trust me," I said, "she's having fun. She gets to punish me for all of this later."

Sashenka's laughter shattered the last of my pensive mood and, waving together at her friends, we headed home.

Chapter Two

A quick shower later and I settled in a deck chair next to the Hensley's pool, the last of the sun sinking into the ocean. As much as I sucked at surfing, I loved the West coast. I'd had to wrangle some concessions out of my vampire core, convincing her to allow me time in the sun. She'd finally caved somewhat, agreeing to most of the morning and from late afternoon on, though she just couldn't bear the heat and full sunlight of midday of the California summer.

Fair enough. I could compromise. Honest.

I even managed a little bit of a tan, amazing. Being part vampire had its uses, even better since I wasn't tied completely to the whole turn to ash in the sun lifestyle. But the thought of going through the rest of eternity without a tan actually made me a little weepy.

Vanity, thy name is Syd.

Sashenka sank into the deck chair beside me with a huge grin, her wet hair in a rough bun at the nape of her neck, dark skin shining in the sunset. "These past two weeks went by so fast." She reached out and took my hand. "I had so much fun, Syd."

Me too. "I can't believe you liked Wilding Springs," I said. She'd come to my place first, spending time in the nuthouse. Willingly. Brave girl. "With a place like this to live?" I drew a deep breath. Yup, could get used to it.

Too bad I was tied to the Wild Hunt in my back yard and could never leave Wilding Springs, our coven magic linked to it until the end of days.

Way to bum yourself out, idiot.

Sashenka rolled her eyes. "Trust me, this place can get old fast."

Right. The clubs and the parties and the food and the endless summer. Compared to humdrum, boring, oh my swearword we're going to die, yawnfest. And cold. I shivered in the sun at the memory of snow.

Just seemed like sacrilege to even consider going home.

Sashenka sighed and stared into the red horizon. "I was happy to have you here," she said. "But even more so to see where you live." She flashed her very white teeth in a smile. "Your family is so amazing. And it was nice to see Liam." She flushed a little. "Not like that or anything."

Oh dear.

"It's cool," I said. "We're not together." So why did saying it make my stomach clench into a knot of "hell no she couldn't have him"? "Remember?"

She nodded a little, biting her lower lip. "I still don't get it," she sniffed. "He's so... you know. And Quaid is such a..." She thumped both hands down on the arms of her chair. I had, naturally, in a fit of poor me, told her everything that happened between Quaid and I between moment one and the present ignoring of each other.

"Yeah," I said, thinking of his little friend Payten and her big rack and how I'd love to hurt her. Just a little. "Whatever."

"On the other hand," she cast me a wicked look, "how about that Sebastian? I know he's a vampire and all but, yowza. I was happy to lay my eyes on him again."

I snorted, my turn to blush. Sashenka and I had both been present when he'd addressed the Council during Mom's trial, his deliciously sexy body covered, if you could call it that, in the barest of fabric scraps.

I still had naughty dreams about him.

Giggling like a little kid, I kicked her chair as she waggled her eyebrows at me.

"Stop," I choked. "I can't breathe."

She rolled sideways, smiling at me, hand under her cheek. "You just have so much cool stuff at home," she said. Followed my eyes as they swept over the ocean stretched out before us. "Yes, I know," she said. "I'm very lucky. But you have the Wild under your yard," thanks for the reminder, "a hound, a demon cat," true, very true, "a sweet younger sister who is half demon," I missed Meira with a sudden pang of pain when Sashenka brought her up, "a Sidhe cavern full of amazing books," not mine, but I got her point, "a vampire and witch family, the most amazing of all is your grandmother, Ethpeal." Sigh. Gram. "A whole demon plane to explore when you decide to go back." Not going to happen willingly, but whatever. "And," she poked my foot with one finger, "a maji historical archive to dig around in."

When she put it that way, I felt homesick. "Thanks," I said. "You're right."

She shrugged, looked away again, face falling from a smile to sadness. "I don't mean to be ungrateful either," she said, volume of her voice dropping as she went on. "I guess I'm just restless."

Hmmm. "What do you mean?" Was it wrong my mind went immediately to Gram and her insistence I find a second? She'd been badgering me lately, saying she wanted to pass on the family magic sooner rather than later, so she could have some kind of retirement. And don't get me wrong, she'd absolutely earned one. But even if I could bear the thought of not having her right there with me all the time, there was no one in my coven I felt comfortable having as a second.

And don't think Sashenka hadn't crossed my mind as a candidate once I realized I had to look outside the family. But she was already filling the role for her sister, Tallah. Off limits, in my opinion.

Nothing mattered more than family.

"I've never lived anywhere but here." Sashenka spread her arms. "We've never had to leave, isn't that weird?"

I guess. I'd moved about a million times in my childhood thanks to some magical indiscretion forcing us to pack up and take off in the middle of the night. More for the protection of the normals around us than because of any risk to the family.

"California." Sashenka grinned, the light coming back into her face. "Everybody is so into themselves here, no one notices a little weirdness." She paused. "I wish I could go home with you."

"Me too." Though I really wished I could stay. But I had to go back, to prepare for school in a few weeks, but more so to get ready for Uncle Frank and Sunny's wedding. The vampire pair were so excited, and Sunny chose me as her maid of honor.

No way I was missing it.

"You could come back with me," I said, but Sashenka shook her head even as I spoke.

"It's cool," she said. "I'll see you at school anyway."

"Are you having trouble with Tallah?" I didn't want

to ask. It wasn't my business. And it could have been seen as interference in another coven. Big no-no. But Sashenka didn't take it the wrong way, like I knew she wouldn't.

"It's not that." Her voice dropped to a whisper. "I would just like to get out there on my own for once. School's been a bad influence." Sashenka squeezed my hand. "And so have you. I'm seeing there's more to life than being my sister's second."

"You want to lead a coven?" I knew it happened, how some witches broke free of their families for various reasons to start their own little communities. But Sashenka's snort told me I was off base.

"Not," she laughed. "But I don't know if I want to be in Tallah's shadow the rest of my life, either. Not when it feels like I'm her choice out of duty."

Don't do it, Syd. Don't. Do. It.

Ah, crap.

"Speaking of which," I said, all casual like. "Gram's been after me to choose a second of my own. In prep for her handing over the rest of the family magic."

Sashenka met my eyes, hers full of questions. "Really," she said.

"Yup." I was going to hell. No way I could break up a happy family.

No way.

The glitter in Sashenka's eyes did amazing things to my resolve. And maybe we would have said or planned things we shouldn't have, if we'd been left to do so.

Fortunately—I think—we were interrupted. Tallah strode out into the cooling evening with a big smile, her power preceding her as she crashed our little party.

"You girls have fun?" Only a few years older, but already a force to be reckoned with, Tallah was my only real friend among the other coven leaders. Guilt drove me to my feet and to hug her.

"Had a great day," I said, smiled as I pulled away. "And an amazing vacation. Thank you for having me."

Her answering smile was open, honest. "Our pleasure, Syd," she said, holding out her hand to Sashenka. My bestie took it, coming to stand next to her sister, head down, shoulders a little slumped. "Any time. Right, Shenka?" Tallah hugged her with one arm, apparently unaware of how Sashenka's mood shifted.

Then again, Sashenka always acted the same way around Tallah. So maybe the older Hensley had no idea. And I wasn't in any position just yet to make a formal request. If Sashenka even considered joining my coven as a possibility.

Charlotte appeared over Tallah's shoulder, motioned for me.

Right. Time to go. I hugged both of my friends again and turned to pick up a bag. Which Charlotte immediately liberated. I reached for another, only to have it pulled from my grasp. Who were we, the Two Stooges? I rolled my eyes at her before hugging Sashenka again on impulse.

Whispered in her ear. "We'll talk at school."

Her eyes lit up and she grinned like I'd given her a gift.

Definitely going to hell.

Chapter Three

The edge of the park was wreathed in night when Charlotte and I stepped out of the veil on the other side of the family wards. One look around at the dark houses on my street and I groaned. It was three hours later here, well after midnight.

Time zones sucked.

That meant everyone was sleeping. I'd have to save hugs and hellos and gift giving for the morning. It also meant, to be fair, we had to be quiet going in. Hard to do when my family magic yearned for the center of my coven's power, Shaylee sinking herself into the ground to check on Gwynn and the Wild while my demon yammered to see Meira and Sassafras. At least my vampire, as quiet and calm as ever, didn't prod me.

I appreciated her for her stoic nature. At least one of us had her head screwed on straight.

Charlotte held the door for me, winding her way down the hall and up the stairs without a backward look. Leaving me to have a heart-to-heart with the fluffy silver Persian waiting for me at the back door. Sassafras stood up on his hind legs, front paws on my thigh. I immediately obliged his request for up and lifted him into my arms. I snuggled him against me, inhaling the scent of his soft fur while he purred in my ear so loudly I expected Gram's door to slam open any second. I hurried past her room and to the stairs, avoiding the creaky step. I really needed to fix it. All it would take was a touch of magic, but I was so used to the step now, avoiding it seemed easier than repair.

Charlotte stood in my room when I arrived, dumping my bags on the bed before turning her back on me with a grunt. Still pissed, huh? Oh, well. She'd get over it.

She always did.

"I take it you've managed to irritate Charlotte again." Sassafras didn't miss a thing. I sat down on the edge of the bed amid my vacation belongings to give his mane a good scratch. Sassy's amber eyes closed over in a slow blink as his purr grew louder, whole body bending into my hand.

"Just a little accident," I said, keeping it mild.

His head snapped up, purr cut off in an instant. "What did you do?"

I laughed and set him down. "Nothing," I said,

choice."

He licked my fingers. "It will all work out the way it's meant to," he said. "If I've learned nothing since I've joined your coven, it's that you Hayle witches seem to attract only the best and, despite the difficulties, you always end up stronger than before."

He was right. Like we had a handful of horseshoes shoved in various places.

"Your grandmother missed you, by the way," he said, voice sleepy as his eyes drifted closed. "And Liam. Fool boy was here with that hound every day asking about you."

Um hum. I leaned close and kissed his soft forehead, rubbing my cheek against his silky fur.

"I missed you too," I said.

Grunt. One eye winked and closed again.

Smiling with tears standing behind my eyes, I fell asleep.

"Sydlynn," Sebastian drew me into his powerful arms, draping me backward, the open throat of my ball gown offering up the smooth skin of my neck to his glistening fangs. "I've loved you for so long. I can't bear to be apart."

"My lord," I breathed, gazing into his smoldering eyes, my body burning for his touch, breasts aching to burst forth from the bindings of my corset. "I'm yours forever."

His mouth descended, the heat of his breath bringing a gasp of pleasure from my lips as liquid fire poured through my body, setting aflame parts of me begging for release—

"Syd."

A sharp nail prodded my cheek.

"Syd, wakey."

Gasp. What?

My eyes flashed open, locked on a pair of faded blue ones hovering so close I could barely focus on Gram's grinning face.

"Breakfast." She bounced in excitement, leaning on her elbows, hands in front of her mouth as her eyes danced with delight. "Up!"

She giggled as she stood up, turning in a happy, dancing circle, fuzzy socks silent on my carpet as she jigged her way to the door where she paused and pointed at me with the same offending digit, bending it in summons.

"Up!"

Okay, okay. I waved at her as she shimmied away, humming a tune to which only she knew the words, falling back into my pillow while my body complained at the interruption of my dream.

Blushing. I pressed both palms to my hot cheeks and bit my lower lip, a nervous giggle escaping. Oh dear.

It was hard enough meeting Sebastian's eyes knowing what I did about his anatomy, but even worse when fantasy intruded without my permission.

One very cold shower later and I could face Gram, though I yawned my way down the stairs and to the kitchen, body still on West coast time.

Gram happily deposited a plate of Eggs Benedict at my place, where juice and milk already waited for me. I ignored the food, going to her, hugging her though she was busy dishing up her own meal, feeling her arms around me, spatula held high.

"Love you," I whispered. "I missed you."

She didn't say anything, but when I pulled away and met her eyes, they brimmed with tears. She grinned at me though, before filling her own plate and joining me at the table. Charlotte was already seated, waiting for us to start before beginning her own breakfast, silent and watchful as ever, while Sassafras noisily snuffled up the last of his tuna before tackling the cream in his china bowl.

Family. Awesome.

Why wasn't I surprised when Liam showed up, Galleytrot in tow? The big black hound licked my face when I hugged him. Liam didn't care I wiped the slobber off on the shoulder of his t-shirt.

Another plate of eggs appeared, a bowl of fresh meat.

More family. Sashenka was right. This was my home and I loved it here.

"I've been doing a ton of research on the maji," Liam started yammering between giant bites of breakfast.

"Sebastian's been letting me practically camp out in the history room."

The vampire's visit in my dreams leaped to my mind with the reminder. Blush. Damn it. If Liam noticed, he didn't say.

We ended up outside on the bench after Gram shooed us away, her magic dealing with the dishes. Liam finally wound down about his research before flushing himself and taking my hand.

"Sorry, I haven't let you get in a word. How was your trip?"

Funny, I didn't feel like talking about it. "Fun," I said, softening the single word answer with a smile. "I missed home."

His answering smile told me I'd somehow managed to lead him on again.

"We missed you," he said. Stood up. "I should go."

Awkward. "Liam—"

He didn't give me notice, warning, nothing. Just bent over me, his warm lips pressing to mine, hands gentle and tentative on my shoulders. I found myself kissing him back as much as I knew it was a bad idea, leaning into his soft t-shirt, the fragrance of earth and fabric softener Liam's signature for me. I think I could have found him in the dark just by his distinct scent alone.

When he finally released me, my whole body tingled and I swayed a little. Earth magic was powerful stuff.

Liam stroked his thumb over my lips before offering a lop-sided smile, green glinting in his hazel eyes.

"Love you," he whispered before turning and loping off.

I heard a grunt, turned to see Galleytrot push his way through the screen door and past me, eyes flickering with red fire as he met mine on the way by.

Like it was my fault. Liam wouldn't listen to reason. And yes, I should have been more firm about the whole no-boyfriend thing. But he was relentless in his sweet and kind-hearted way.

But how could I link myself to him when I was turning into something that scared the crap out of me?

Chapter Four

If there were indeed levels of hell, doing laundry was one of them. I shoved a half-dozen pair of wadded up underwear into a drawer and said good enough. Who folded that stuff, anyway?

I kicked the basket into my closet and closed the door before sinking to my bed with a sigh. Now for a nice, quiet afternoon catching up on my favorite book series—romance fanatic? Guilty—and snack on junk while ignoring the world for one more day.

Alas, the best laid plans. How quickly life returned to normal.

With a rush of power, three witches passed through the family wards, two of them tied to the coven's magic. The other one was still welcome by the power living in the house, though. Acceptable since she'd spent most of her life as part of the coven.

I could hardly blame the family magic for welcoming my mother home.

Bouncing down to greet them seemed a little over the top, but despite my previous expectations of the day to the contrary, I was really happy for the distraction. Until I spotted the bags, boxes and bows Erica and Mom loaded onto the kitchen table before Mom opened her arms to me for a hug.

"Oh no," I whispered in her ear. "Sunny's shower." How much did I suck? Here I was, maid of honor, and I'd forgotten the *shower*.

Bad, Syd. Bad, bad, bad.

Mom laughed and kissed my cheek, hers pale and a little drawn though her eyes were merry.

"I wanted you to have a nice vacation," Mom said, stepping away so Meira could hug me too. My little sister had grown again, her chin the height of my shoulder now. She was like the amazing stretching girl, her face maturing much faster than I liked. She'd been away most of the summer at Harvard, taking her extra training, so I forgot how fast she was growing up since she returned from Demonicon. Only eleven years old eleven and a half if you asked her—she now looked fifteen.

I'd be beating off the boys with magic-drenched sticks in the next little while.

"Hey, Meems." Her right horn poked my cheek as she turned her head to smile up at me.

"Hey, Syd," she said. "We brought everything, so don't worry."

"All under control." Erica Plower, Mom's former second and now the Hayle coven representative on the Council, tossed back her blonde bob and winked, her cropped jacket and skinny jeans every inch the woman I knew. Mom might have still clung to the old ways with her floor-length black velvet skirts and puffy silk blouses, but Erica embraced what was current and hip.

I just wished my butt looked that good. Sigh.

Where once I would have dreaded family time, I found myself laughing and enjoying myself as we all pitched in to decorate the back yard. Even Gram got into the swing, though the embarrassingly shaped balloons she created were quickly popped while we all giggled like mad and Gram cackled with her hands on her knees and her eyes snapping with mischief.

If Meira was blushing she hid it well behind her human facade. Because I know I was.

Mom winked as she looked up, the soft gray clouds hovering over us twitching in the dying light of the afternoon. No, it wasn't really legal to mess with the weather, but I wasn't about to say anything for ensuring we'd have a dry and pleasant evening.

I had just enough time to dash upstairs and change into a sundress and sandals, stuffing Sunny's present into the gift bag I'd bought and drenching it in fancy paper before the feeling of more people arriving drove me downstairs to play hostess.

Weird, but fun and kind of gratifying, too. This was my first real experience with being a grown up when it came to having people over and, I'm happy to say, I wasn't as nervous as I expected. And yes, this whole shindig was my idea. The moment I had a chance, I jumped online and did some research into my duties, quickly filling in Mom, Erica and Meira who were instantly on my side and eager to help. Good thing, or this whole shower would have consisted of me standing in the kitchen with a lame excuse to explain why I'd forgotten once I mentioned it.

Maybe my week spent relaxing in California did help though, considering I usually wasn't all that confident around the family unless there was a major disaster to tackle, but it was more likely my new-found appreciation for the people in my life the real culprit.

A stream of witches arrived first, younger members and older, all women. Naturally. Female witches and vampires were as excitable as the next girl when it came to a good bridal shower.

By the time the sun finally set, the back yard was full of chattering, laughing witches sipping drinks and snacking on hors d'oeuvres as I anxiously checked my watch for the time.

"They'll be here soon," Mom said, tipping her glass to

me. "This was a lovely idea, sweetheart. The perfect way to welcome Sunny into our family." Was it hard for her to sit back and let me run the party? She didn't show it, if that was the case.

I loved my mom.

And then, with a shudder of shadow, the vampires began to arrive, flooding the yard with their glowing white power as they eagerly came forward to hug and mingle with the family. I found myself grinning at the spectacle, feeling my heart swell. Yes, we were allies and had been for some time, but ever since Sebastian's clan joined us in the fight against the Brotherhood, carrying the coven in partnership to do battle against a common enemy, the bond between our two people had firmed up. Old walls shattered, friendships formed between witch and vampire until I felt like my family had grown by another hundred people or so.

Who cared if they were undead? I'd take them in a heartbeat.

Mine. Since they didn't have one. Whatever.

When Sunny appeared at last, Anastasia beside her, I rushed forward and hugged her, feeling her wrap herself around me in return. The second blonde vampire, one of Sebastian's most trusted lieutenants, stepped aside, allowing us space, though with good humor for once. It took her a long time to warm up to me, even worse since I carried the vampire essence inside me, but despite our last uncomfortable run-in she seemed much more relaxed and even smiled my way.

Not that I was really paying attention. Sunny gave the best hugs. Whole body squeezes telling me with no uncertainty how much she loved me. Her beautiful face lit up when she turned from our embrace to look over the crowd now watching her, as I leaned inside the house and turned on the lights.

I could have used magic. But we had neighbors. So the strings of white bulbs and floating gauze fabrics Mom and Erica brought would have to do. Sunny gasped and covered her mouth with her hands, turning to me with a smile and tears in her eyes.

"Syd," she whispered. "Thank you."

The applause greeting her when she stepped forward made my heart sing.

If anyone deserved to be happy, it was Sunny and my Uncle Frank. Sunny was welcomed and the party really started. Though I watched Mom's face as she hugged Sunny around the shoulders and saw her eyes fill with tears.

I knew she was thinking about Dad. So was I. Meira too, from the hug she gave Mom. Their pairing severed and his ass firmly in the Second Seat of Demonicon, Dad's departure left a hole in all of our lives, but none more so than Mom's.

She smiled at both Meems and me, kissed us as she

shooed us away. "I'm fine," she said. "I promise. This is a happy night. Let's make sure Sunny knows we're thrilled to have her join our family."

Did we. Gifts and funny stories and games filled the evening, bows and ribbon torn from packages stuck to Sunny's hair. I nervously waited for her reaction to her present, unsure if I'd made the right choice. But when she held up the carefully secured pentagram necklace inside its blue velvet box, smiling at me like the sun coming up, I knew I'd done okay.

Tied to my magic, like the one I wore was tied to Mom, Sunny would now have a piece of me everywhere she went.

Which reminded me. I glanced Mom's way, finding her neck bare. She really must not have liked the new one Meira and I bought her to replace the necklace she lost. I tried not to feel hurt, focusing on the smiling vampire.

"I love you, too," Sunny whispered, voice catching as she hugged me, the pentagram warm between us. "Sister."

I grinned at her. "Um, niece."

That made her laugh.

"Last game of the evening." Erica held out a blindfold with a wicked grin. "Hide and seek, bride to be."

Sunny accepted the challenge. The moment she had her back turned, we all scattered. Well, not all of us. Some of the older witches remained behind, still chattering with their vampire friends but, for the most part, we took off for the park and dove for cover.

I had the perfect spot picked out. The grove where she and I once talked, when I'd asked her to make me a vampire. Memory ran through me in a shudder, of the girl I was then, powerless and afraid for my family. That night, Sunny showed me a different side of her, the warrior inside the beautiful and giving vampire I already loved. Her strength helped me through one of the hardest times in my life.

I wondered if she remembered.

The only crimp in my style? Charlotte hovered next to me, as always, totally ruining my chances of hiding. Sunny may have been blindfolded, but no way would her heightened vampire senses miss a combo of witch, demon, vampire and Sidhe being clung to by a werewolf.

I hissed at my bodywere who scowled back at me. Still miffed, clearly. Too freaking bad. If she chose to be a wet blanket and not enjoy herself, that was Charlotte's decision. I waved her off, watched as she relented, drifting a little way away to hide behind another tree. Not far enough for my liking and still close enough she could keep an eye on me, but it would have to do.

Squealing echoed from further away. I found myself giggling, holding my hand over my mouth to keep in my nervous excitement. I had it all worked out. The moment

Sunny tried to tag me I was going to dive into the veil and hide elsewhere. No way was she going to catch me.

Shadow flickered next to me, the rush of a vampire arriving making me laugh. I turned, mock anger on my face, to accuse Sunny of cheating.

Only to stop, shocked. Look up. Into a face I knew. But not the one I expected.

Charlotte's howl behind me didn't come fast enough. Piotr, the vampire I'd met thanks to Ameline Benoit and a crap-ton of trouble, blew a handful of white powder into my face. I inhaled with a gasp as I drew breath in surprise, choking on the dust just as I felt Sebastian's mind reach for mine.

Sydlynn!

Too late, all of them too late despite their supernatural speed. I felt Charlotte's hand brush over the back of my dress as the world shuddered and went black.

Chapter Five

Poke. *Wake up.*

Grumble, mumble.

Poke, poke. *You must wake.*

Sigh. Breath.

Gasp.

I sat up and shot to my feet in the same motion, staggering as I fought for balance. But my physical body didn't matter.

Didn't.

Not when I couldn't feel my magic.

Correction. Not all of it. Demon? Missing. Shaylee? Nowhere to be felt. Vampire?

Yes, she sent. *I'm here with you.*

Relief and panic and fear and burning rage heating to eruption warred inside me as I looked up and around the small stone room with the low slung bed and a black wool blanket. I saw the tall, thin window, old rippled glass looking out over what looked like mountains, a fat and heavy moon shining in on me.

Mountains?

A door squatted in the middle of the far wall. Thick and wooden, wider than I was used to, a round knob in the center of rough black iron begged to be turned. I stormed my way forward. Started to. Tripped over the rough rock under my feet, caught on the edge of the woven mat beside the bed. I just managed to catch myself from falling over.

Someone was going to pay with their life.

The knob felt icy in my hand, and resisted my attempts to turn it. Locked, huh? We'd see about that. I reached for my demon to shatter it into a million pieces.

Had to clench my fists around the jab of absolute terror I felt when she didn't answer me.

She can't. The vampire sighed. *They've been neutralized, both of them. Demon and Sidhe, and your family magic with them. But you have me.*

Yes. Yes. Gratitude returned in a rush. I reached out for Gram, for Mom. Anyone.

I can't feel them, the vampire sent. *But there are those I do know.*

Sebastian. I felt him faintly, somewhere out there beyond the doorway. Shielded against me, had to be. And

Sunny, the momentary touch of her love. Uncle Frank.

I wasn't alone.

Knowing that went a long way toward helping me calm down. The initial rush of adrenaline burned off, I drew a deep breath, resting my head against the thickly grained wood of the oak door, forcing myself to calm, calm.

Calm.

Better, she sent, the vampire's tone soothing. *Much better.*

What's happening? Coherent. Good for me.

I don't know for certain, she answered.

The white powder. I knew the stuff. Had been under its influence before when Demetrius Strong used it to cut off my power before the cherubic leader of the Chosen of the Light tied me to a stake and tried to burn me alive.

Horror fluttered around my heart with the wings of a desperate bird, driving my calm away again.

My vampire went on, tone sharper. *Pull yourself together. We're not in Wilding Springs anymore.*

I choked on a half-hysterical laugh. *Does that make my demon the lion, Shaylee the scarecrow and you the tin man looking for a heart?*

She didn't say anything for a long time, though her confusion came throug so clear I couldn't hold in the giggle taking over.

I don't know what that means, she finally sent. *This isn't funny.*

I know. I stepped back from the door and hugged myself. *I'm sorry. Nerves. We have to get out of here.* My claustrophobia ramped up as I faced the unyielding exit. Not that the room was tiny or anything, not at all. But the feeling of being trapped would still have clung to me even if it was three times its size.

Agreed, she sent. *The door is locked.*

Oh. My. Swearword. The giggles again.

Really, she snapped. *This is no time for hysterics.*

Cut me a little slack, I sent back. *I take it you have an idea about the lock? Some secret vampire magic that can cut through the door?*

Of course not, she sent. *Why bother when we can teleport out of here?*

Okay then.

Right, I sent. *Just teleport. Gotcha. How do I do that again?*

She sighed heavily. *You're not normally this dense*, she sent.

It's been a rough night. Sarcasm back in place? Check. *Just show me what to do already.*

It was surprisingly easy. Just a shift in body mass, spirit magic sliding between atoms, my body turning to a kind of floating mist. I hovered there, the world around me black-edged and cold while my vampire observed.

Excellent, she sent. *Now, think of where you want to go.*

Home? That would be awesome.

No, she sent. *The wards on this castle prevent you leaving using vampire magic.*

I reached out with my demon... sigh.

Okay, I sent. *I'll believe you.*

Oh, thank you, she sent. *Thank you, thank you.*

When did she become so snarky? And why did I think it was my influence?

We're in this together, I shot back.

I know. She shuddered inside me. *I'm sorry. We're both on edge. Close your eyes and see.*

I did. Cool. There was still a door, but it was transparent, the wall, too. A pair of glowing white shapes stood on the other side, black holes up high which had to be windows. And a hallway.

Shall we? She prodded me gently as I focused on being there and went.

Flickering out of shadow and into the light on the other side of the door.

Wicked.

I spun to face the two vampire guards who stared at me in shock.

"Hiya," I waved a little. "Air's a little stuffy in there."

My vampire hissed softly. At her urging, I turned around to see a familiar form half-running toward me, his face creased in his own brand of shock.

"Piotr," I said, anger rising again at last. "You asshole."

My vampire reacted with me, driving me forward even though I didn't need the encouragement, slamming into him and driving him backward. The vampire tried to shudder out of my grip, but the essence inside me held him as I grasped the front of his elaborate jacket in my hands and jerked his face down to my level.

"You have a lot of explaining to do," I snarled. Paused. "And dying. After the explaining."

Piotr shook his head. "You shouldn't have access to power."

Underestimated me, did he? "You have no idea who you're dealing with, clearly." I let my vampire out, feeling my teeth lengthen, the cold of her chilling me to the bone, the heat of my anger now a slowly sharpening blade of ice. "This is the last time you screw with a Hayle."

Sydlynn! Sebastian's mind touched mine. *Don't harm him.*

Oh, hell no. *Says who?* The need to tear Piotr apart for his arrogance almost won.

There is more to this than you know. Sadness, concern. *Please. You must listen.*

Fine. I let Piotr go with a savage smile, shoving him from me with a certain amount of power behind my gesture. He stepped back a pace, the usual vampire grace returning the moment he was out of my grip.

"I'm under orders," he said, like that made one tiny little miniscule bit of difference.

Sebastian's mind hovered in mine as I thought it over. "Whoever gave you those orders is about to be damned sorry." I shoved past him, making it about three steps before I turned back to find him staring at me with sullen rage. "Well, errand boy? Are you coming or sulking?"

Oh snap.

I allowed him to lead me, needing the time to let my mind absorb what I'd learned. A) I was out of my element and country, quite likely. B) My friends were here, but only the vampire ones, from what I could tell. And C) I only had access to vampire magic.

Bit of a change from the last time I was conscious.

Sebastian. I didn't mean to snap at him, but if he didn't forgive me for being short under the circumstances, he could bite me. *Why am I even here? Why was I kidnapped? What the hell is going on?*

Ah, hell.

You're safe, he sent back, though his whole tone tipped me off he wasn't being a hundred per cent honest. *For now.*

Nice. At least I wasn't under the control of the bad vampires. Or the ones I considered bad. Nicholas's clan, Sebastian's dead brother, had a terrible reputation he'd earned fair and square as far as I was concerned. And considering Piotr, a clan mate of Nicholas, had been part of Ameline's plan to use normals in some kind of ritual to increase her power, I tended to agree with my first assessment.

If Sebastian and clan were present, I had to have a fighting chance against whatever was going on. Surely they'd back me.

Wouldn't they?

And I needed said backing why?

Too many questions. But Sunny wasn't reachable, Uncle Frank either, lost behind some spirit wall my vampire couldn't break and Sebastian had gone suddenly quiet.

I was about to prod Piotr for information when two giant wooden doors swung open in front of me and vampires surrounded me.

Talk about walking into the dragon's den.

Chapter Six

It felt like I'd been dropped into a medieval film set. Both sides of the vast room lined with vampires, a black runner bisecting the room to the two large wooden chairs—thrones, actually—at the other end of the space. A massive, round, stained-glass window took up most of the back wall. A moment of study made me shudder and look away from the violence depicted, a scene in stunning glass of death and destruction, blood spilled by vampires.

Guess those were the good old days. Current law didn't allow them to feed from humans, even willing ones, at least not directly. Most clans, from what I'd been told by Sunny and Uncle Frank, had human servants who served as mobile blood banks, keeping the clan in donated nourishment augmented by blood brought in from hospitals and clinics and, occasionally, from animals.

My eyes found Sebastian standing on the left, caught

his gaze and held it a moment, though only a moment. I couldn't help but give him the once over, since he was dressed like some court gentleman in a navy blue velvet frock coat and ruffled white shirt.

Don't even get me started on the tight white pants.

Grrrrowl. Down girl.

It had to be my vampire's fault. No way I'd allow myself to be distracted at a time like this.

Her snort told me I was deluding myself, but I ignored her by choice.

Sunny was another shocker, her floor-length gown shimmering silver, sitting low on her shoulders, showing enough cleavage for the both of us, hair piled artfully in corkscrew curls. Last time I saw her we were celebrating at a bridal shower. So, there had been time to doll themselves up while I snored away in a tiny little room.

Temper, temper. Though I couldn't help the glare I shot at Uncle Frank. He had the good grace to look embarrassed by his own fancy attire.

The other side of the room had to be Piotr's people. At least, that was my guess, considering the glares traveling back and forth over the dividing carpet, though they were rare enough while the two camps watched my approach. Nice of them to offer me a change of clothes. My little sun dress did little to keep the chill off in the damp castle. From the soft flapping sound, one of my new sandal's edge had peeled away from the sole. And I knew my hair had to be a fright.

Hey, I stood out.

Go me.

Appearances seemed important to these people. The two women—okay, vampires—on the thrones I approached were as elaborately decked out as their clans, more so. Which made me think of Ahbi Sanghamitra and the demon court. Leading me to irritation and anger at the posturing. So by the time I stood at the bottom of the wooden pedestal, glaring up at the two leaders, I was in no mood for their little show.

I didn't give Piotr a chance to speak, grasping him firmly with my vampire magic and shoving him aside so he staggered and had to catch his balance. The glare of pure hatred he shot at me warmed me up and made me all fuzzy happy.

It's the small things, sometimes.

"You two," I jabbed a finger at the pair of vampires staring down at me like I was a bug they wanted to squash, "better have a damned good reason for kidnapping an American coven leader."

Neither spoke. Didn't matter. I had more to say anyway.

"Not only is this a massive treaty violation," I snarled, just warming up, "but I'm so far outside your jurisdiction, not to mention your league, you'll both be lucky to lead a termite colony when I'm done with you."

So there.

The leader on the left, camp Sebastian, stared at me in silence, her cold gray eyes almost colorless. Her skin shone ivory white, dark brown hair piled around her in endless waves, as long as she was tall. She showed no concern, lovely face expressionless.

The other smirked at me, ice blue eyes sparking with humor, nothing good about it. Dark blonde hair, coiled in wave-like ribbons, hanging over one bare shoulder.

I knew her. From where? And how? Impossible. I'd never met either of the vampire Queens. Had only heard of them through Sebastian. So why was it I had the feeling the vampire on my right knew me, too?

A second vampire stood beside her, a cloak covering her dress, hood low over her face. But the sinking feeling of pre-knowledge grew stronger as I stared at the two of them, joined by a sickening pinpoint of anxiety.

Who were they?

"We are within our rights." The leader on the left finally spoke, tearing my gaze from the others. I focused on her as she went on, motionless, voice velvet over jagged ice. "You've stolen our power, and we want it back."

Um, what?

Me, Sydlynn, the vampire sent. *They want me.*

Oh, *hell* no.

Sebastian stepped forward, coming to my side, facing

me with a warning in his eyes as I drew a breath to tell her where she could shove her sense of entitlement.

"May I present our Matriarch, first among our familial clan, Queen Pannera Sthol."

What, was I supposed to bow or something? Yeah. Right.

"I wish I could say nice to meet you," I snapped. "Not."

Sebastian's eyes widened just a little bit. The vampire Queen didn't react. Instead, Piotr took his place opposite Sebastian.

"Our Matriarch," he said.

Didn't get to finish.

Not while his Queen was laughing. So. Familiar. I knew the tone, the timber, but it was smoother, softer, more refined. Silkified. The vampire Queen gestured for him to back off, her motions graceful.

"We've already had the pleasure, haven't we, my dear?"

That voice.

No.

Oh no.

Polished or not by her vampire blood, no way could I forget that voice. The sight of Demetrius Strong peeking out from behind her throne told me I was right.

But it couldn't be. How could this stunning blonde possibly—

The tall vampire beside her swept her hood back, smiling at me, horse face no longer ugly, braid now a rippling, living cape of chestnut hair. She'd changed too, Celeste Oberman had. Not the woman, the witch, I remembered. Swore to kill.

Gorgeous, young, vital, as though the vampire spirit magic had brought her to full potential.

"Welcome, Sydlynn," Batsheva Moromond said. "It's time to hand over what belongs to me."

Chapter Seven

I know it was childish, but the first thought to cross my mind after their identities sank in was how unfair my life was. Batsheva had been a dumpy, chubby woman with fake, dark blonde hair and weak blue eyes, face lined with those creases around her lips that made lipstick bleed.

And Celeste? Yeah, horse-faced was my best description for the traitor the last time I'd seen her, the braid a thick weave of brown and threads of gray, reminding me of an equine tail.

How come the moment they became vampires they were suddenly gorgeous? Celeste looked like an Amazon, but in a beautiful way, wide jaw now appealing, brown eyes with a hint of gold, her youth returned to her. And Batsheva?

Drop dead hotness. At least, on the outside. No

amount of spirit magic could make her attractive on the inside.

My vampire sighed. *You have no idea, do you?*
What?

Regardless of my internal conversation, the world went on without me. Namely, the furious reaction Pannera had to Batsheva's little statement. I'd always thought of vampires as just folks, growing up with one for an uncle and his sweet girlfriend, loving and kind. Rarely did I get to see them in their unhappy, going-to-bite-you state.

Pannera had no trouble showing she was pissed. Fangs sprouted from her mouth. Not just her canines, but all of her teeth lengthening to pinpoints of deadly whiteness. Her eyes flared with power, skin so transparent her veins stood out in sharp contrast, pulsing despite the fact her heart didn't beat.

She only showed a moment of her displeasure, but it was enough for me.

Guess I wasn't the only one with a temper.

"Our power, you mean." Her voice echoed in the stillness her show of anger left behind.

Batsheva sat back, watching the other vampire Queen with hooded eyes, a slight smile still on her ruby lips. "It remains to be seen who will be strong enough to take and hold it, my dear Pannera."

Nice of them to talk about divvying me up like that.

Let them try. In the meantime, I had my own questions to be answered.

"What happened to the other Queen?" I already knew. Batsheva was nothing if not predictable when it came to grabbing for power. Nothing but absolute dominance would do.

Yvette Wilhelm, Sebastian sent.

Nicholas's creator. I'd never had the full story from Sebastian, how he and his brother ended up at odds. The blood clan leader would never talk about it and, to be honest, so much happened between the time Sebastian took Nicholas down and now, I'd forgotten to ask.

Going to resolve that little oversight the minute I had him alone.

Pannera's face returned to marble perfection while Batsheva tapped her long nails on the arm of her chair with irritating tick-tick-tick sounds.

"I killed her, of course," Batsheva said. "Drained her blood and her power." A few of the vampires on her side shifted, a thin wave of unease reaching me.

Not all support their new Queen it seems, my vampire sent.

Batsheva ignored their reactions, spreading her arms wide as she swept to her feet, golden gown in frothing layers a perfect match for the rich shade of her hair, though the fact she was falling out of the front made me a little nauseous. "I now reign as Queen of the Moromonds."

Talk about melodrama. "How nice for you," I said, not rolling my eyes. Not. Rolling. Them. "How's that working out?"

Exultant joy turned to rage in a flash. "Arrogant child." Me, arrogant? Had she done a serious personal assessment lately? "How dare you!"

Whatever. This was so old even immortal me was feeling the weight of it.

"Listen up," I said, arms crossed over my chest, glaring back and forth between the two Queens, "the pair of you seem to have some facts all screwy."

Sebastian looked like he was going to choke on my irreverence and spun to face his leader. "If I may," he said in his suave voice, giving me an ideal sight line to the way his muscular thighs filled out his tight, white pants, the roundness of his very fine butt just visible under the tails of his coat.

I really had to focus.

Sebastian dove into the story of Cesard and the battle for control over the essence while my vampire very firmly took me in hand, forcing me to focus on something other than Sebastian's body.

I refuse to give myself up to either of these vampires. No uncertainty whatsoever.

Well, I'm with you there, I sent back. *Not only would it be a very bad idea to offer them access to the amount of power you represent, you've kind of grown on me.*

Agreed, she sent, rather softly. It didn't matter how almighty she was, the fact she was ages old and brilliant in many ways, she just didn't get my sense of humor. Oh well. Not many did, even those bonded to me.

I need to neutralize this damned hold over my others. Again anxiety crawled through me when I thought of my demon, Shaylee, the family magic. But not as bad this time, more under control. Though I knew I could turn rabid at any moment and preferred not to drop on all fours and chew the carpet in frustration.

Or on one of the vampires. Pretty sure that would get me in trouble.

We will free all of us, she sent, anger bubbling white and cold, the feeling of her emerging fangs distinct. *And when we do, we will destroy any who dare treat us so*.

Hmm. My vampire side had always been so reserved. Interesting to see her all wound up.

Even more interesting would be watching her cut loose when the time was right.

"Which is when Sydlynn found me." Sebastian turned to me, gesturing for me to finish, but it took me a moment to understand he'd reached the end of his particular part of the story. I really had to learn to pay attention.

I finished the explanation, Sebastian's freedom, Uncle Frank's healing. Pannera and Batsheva both seemed very interested in the fact Uncle Frank was whole again. Like I cared what made them tick. I wrapped up in my typical aggressive manner, refusing to pull punches.

"If it wasn't for Piotr," I said, purposely ignoring him though I could see him snarl at me out of the corner of my eye, "working with Ameline Benoit to enslave normals—a serious crime, by the way, which I'm sure you know—the power you're after would still be trapped inside the gem my father made." I turned and pointed at Piotr at last, pouring on the scorn. "His meddling created this mess."

He pulled back, head down, as though expecting a blow.

But I wasn't done.

"But if you're looking for the real culprit in all of this disaster," I said, "look no further than the venerable Queen Batsheva herself." She had taken her throne again as Sebastian started his side of the tale and now ignored me, examining her fingernails. "If she and her husband hadn't cracked the seal on the demon prison, none of you would even be aware the vampire essence existed."

And I would still be trapped, she whispered to me. *And lost in insanity. Is it wrong I'm grateful?*

No, I sent back. *But I had to say it.*

Pannera bobbed her head slowly as I spoke and, for a moment, I wondered if the end to this laughable confrontation could actually be over so easily.

Leave it to Batsheva to gloss over the facts.

"What you've told us is neither here nor there," she said. "All that matters now is you, a witch, have something you have no right to. The heritage of our race," her voice vibrated with emotion, one hand pressing to her heart as though she really believed the tripe she was handing out, "has been stolen by a child who cares nothing for others, only herself. If you did," she pinned me with her blue eyes, "you would do the right thing and relinquish that which doesn't belong to you."

I'd had enough. "Who says?" *Ready for a show?* I didn't wait for my vampire to answer, just opened up and let her out.

I wished I could see myself. From the looks on the faces of the collection of vampires, it was quite the view. Not only was my vampire ready, she was able and all over it. I felt my body flood with white light, my feet lifting from the floor as I hovered, a great glow exuding from every pore. My memory ran to Sebastian and how deliciously dangerous he was when he carried the essence, an Angel of Death, perfect and deadly and absolutely irresistible.

They looked at me that way now, though their desire clearly came from the need to possess what I had. Maybe showing off wasn't such a good idea, but I needed a strong front and putting my cards out there seemed the best way to prove the vampire and I belonged together.

When I settled to the floor, arms dropping to my

sides, it was a long time before anyone spoke. Sebastian watched me with hunger, though the moment he caught me looking he cast his eyes away.

"In case any of you think I have her inside me against her will," I said, "I've just proven otherwise. She chose me, when she had the chance to be with vampires. I wonder why that is?" So frustrating to understand they didn't get it. "Who are you to tell her the choice she made was the wrong one?"

I expected Batsheva to speak up, but Pannera beat her to it. The vampire Queen seemed clearly agitated, her hands clenched around the arms of her throne, leaning forward toward me while power flashed around her in little lightning strikes.

"The essence inside you created all vampires," she snarled. "And we cannot allow that essence to remain in the hands of one who isn't our race."

All their high and mighty excuses went out the window the moment she spoke.

"You don't want her because I have her," I shot back. "Whoever possesses her has the first power." I looked back and forth between them, disgusted, furious and even more determined to keep the vampire with me. "You just want to be Queen of Everyone. You both make me sick."

Sydlynn, Sebastian sent, an edge to his mental voice. *Please, be cautious.*

To hell with cautious. "I'm sick of being pushed

around," I said, taking a step back, turning in a slow circle so I could meet every pair of eyes in the room before spinning back to the Queens. "You want the essence? Fine. Come and take her from me."

Pannera lunged forward, showing her vampireness all over again. Not impressed. Even when Batsheva hissed, oozing out of her seat, heading for the first step while her people snarled and hovered, ready. Waiting for her orders.

I hope you know what you're doing, my vampire sent.

Um. What?

We can take them, I sent. *Right?*

She sighed. *Oh, Sydlynn*, she sent. *You are the most courageous and ridiculous soul I have ever encountered. We will certainly try.*

Uh-oh. Though not the first time I'd overestimated what I could accomplish. But it never stopped me before.

I didn't get a chance to find out if I had bitten off more than I could chew. The moment I let her out again, the air around me shattered in a million pieces, the breath sucked from my lungs as a horde of Enforcers appeared in a clap of thunder above us.

Stunned, sucking in a new batch of oxygen, I stared up at Mom who floated over me, rage crackling.

"So sorry to be late," she said, power behind her words so strong the floor beneath my feet vibrated with it. "Now release my daughter at once."

Chapter Eight

I wish I could say Mom's demand was met with reason, but vampires, it turned out, weren't the most accommodating creatures. In fact, they reacted en masse with shrieking defiance, blurring and rising themselves, wrapped in shadow, ready to start a battle.

From the look on Mom's face, she was okay with that. And while I was infinitely grateful for the backup, no way was I letting her jump into something that could blow up in our faces in more ways than one.

"How dare you interfere?" Pannera rose, her long black hair writhing around her, navy blue gown rippling as though in a stiff wind. "Leave this place at once and never return!"

"Oh, settle down and take a seat, Pannera." Mom wasn't alone. A portly, older woman with a strong, British accent waved at the Queen as if her reaction was commonplace. The vampire hissed at her, but descended, though she didn't sit, probably out of sheer stubbornness. The round woman with the badly curled head of short hair and snapping hazel eyes fixed Batsheva with her stare. "You too, new girl."

Okay, I was going to like this woman, whoever she was.

"You have no right, Margaret," Pannera said, power still snap-crackle-popping around her.

"Correction," the woman said, settling to the ground with a soft grunt, brushing at the front of her black robe while Mom came to a graceful landing beside her. "You are the ones with no rights here. Our treaty means nothing to you any longer, it seems. I'm happy to revoke it and your permission to remain in Europe. My territory." She might have looked like a well-worn administrator, but her no-nonsense manner came through as loud and clear as the surge of power she carried.

Even blocked, I felt it.

"Council Leader Applegate," Batsheva began, only to be cut off.

"I don't care what you have to say." The older woman hiked up her robes and climbed the stairs to stand next to Pannera. "Are you declaring our treaty null and void or not?"

The vampire Queen grumbled to herself but shook her head. "No," she said. "Of course not."

"And you?" Margaret crossed her arms over her chest, wide bust straining behind the black cloak, eyes locked on Batsheva. "Are you about to be ejected from my property?"

Batsheva sat, a smirk on her lips. "I have no intention of breaking the treaty, Council Leader," she said.

"Excellent. Jolly good to hear it." Margaret turned to fix her gaze on me. "You must be Sydlynn, the source of this debacle and a thorny pain in my very broad backside."

"Yes, ma'am," I said.

"This isn't witch council business." Pannera wasn't letting it go no matter what she just told Margaret.

"I'm making it my business." Cloak bunched up again, Margaret descended to my side and gave me the once over, the top of her head barely reaching my chin. "I thought you were a witch and a demon and a few other things. All I feel is vampire."

"I was drugged," I said. "My powers blocked." I turned and pointed at Batsheva. "Her orders."

"Really." Margaret turned from me, toward the offending throne. "More for me to sort out, then, Batsheva?"

I caught Mom's utter shock in my peripheral vision, glanced her way, found her staring at the vampire Queen and then Celeste before her face settled into a mask.

They were in so much trouble.

"Council Leader Applegate." Mom brushed past me to stand on my other side. "This woman is no vampire Queen, but a criminal who is being pursued for trial in my territory. As is her companion, Celeste Oberman."

Neither of them looked very worried, but I held on to hope.

"I would have them turned over to my custody," Mom went on, "for trial and punishment fitting their despicable crimes."

The vampire protest was loud and aggressive. Even Pannera spoke up, Sebastian seeming troubled by her words.

"They are blood clan now," Pannera said, the volume of her voice quieting the others. "Their race supersedes witch law. They can no longer be held accountable for crimes committed when they were alive. Or so our treaty claims."

Sneaky, nasty—

"You're correct," Margaret said. "Sorry, Miriam."

Mom looked like she was going to, at the very least, argue, if not go after the pair with her bare hands, but finally nodded with so much majesty she put both vampires to shame.

"Very well," Mom said. "I will simply take my coven leader and go."

Pannera again. She was getting on my last nerve. "You cannot take her, not while she holds our property."

Property? My vampire reacted with fury, thrashing around inside me. *Property?*

"You had no right to enter my territory illegally," Mom said. Well, snarled, really. "And kidnap one of my coven leaders." She shook just a little, a tiny tremor passing over her. Yup, Mom was pissed.

Margaret frowned down at the floor a moment. "Agreed," she finally pronounced.

Pannera's protests were cut off by a shot of power from the Council Leader. The portly woman scowled, wrinkled face pruning up as she slashed her hand through the air. "Enough. I'm already sick of this. Miriam Hayle is correct. There are diplomatic channels for such cases as these. Those channels are there for a purpose." She gusted out a sigh. "So monstrous disasters like this one won't happen."

"You would have debated our case for years," Batsheva shot back. "Trapped us in your laws and your talking." As if she hadn't used said tactics herself in the past to get what she wanted. Hypocrite. "This child is not only a thief, she is a menace to all magical races and I for one demand the risk she presents us, the powers she has gained through guile and misdirection, be rectified immediately."

Pannera seemed to have bought Batsheva's company line. "The essence will be returned to our people willingly," she said, "or the girl will be stripped and drained of her blood."

Like that was ever going to happen.

Someone, a vampire someone, teleported close to me and I turned, half expecting an attack. Instead, a massive half-wolf, half-human dove for me. Charlotte, her body out of her control with me in danger, leaped from Anastasia's side right for me, skidding to a halt at my feet, extended snout frothing as she snarled and snapped at the vampires around us.

"How dare you bring a werewolf into our presence?" Pannera jabbed one index finger toward me. "Have that abomination killed. At once."

CHAPTER NINE

My vampire reacted before I could, an explosive gust of spirit magic shoving back the advancing undead with murder in their hearts.

"You touch her," the essence said through my mouth, "and you will feel pain the like of which there has never been."

It probably helped the concussion of her attack had knocked most of them back, even leaving Mom and Margaret wobbling a little. The rotund European Council Leader spun on me with anger in her eyes, but Mom was faster.

"Shall we proceed with said diplomatic talks now?" One of her eyebrows arched artfully as she spoke directly to Margaret in a casual tone, as though the vampire Queens weren't of consequence.

My mom was so many kinds of awesome.

Margaret huffed a moment before shrugging. "Very well. I will moderate."

Pannera sat back with a deep frown that did nothing to mar her beauty. "I will attend," she said.

Batsheva looked like she was going to fight me personally only to turn away and sulk. "Wasting time," she muttered. "But fine. Fine. Let's have our little talk and get on with retrieving our property."

Again with the property. My vampire simmered and I knew, no matter what happened, even if Batsheva succeeded, the essence inside me would never accept her. In fact, would likely make the faux Queen's life a living hell. Though as much as that would serve her right, the end result of such revenge would be me without my vampire side.

Unacceptable.

Margaret led the way out, stomping a path down the middle of the room, gesturing grumpily at the vampires around her though they backed off the moment she came close. Pannera swept after her, Batsheva following close behind, stopping for a moment to come face-to-face with Mom.

"Showing your age these days, Miriam, dear," she said before laughing and striding off.

Mom turned to me, took my hand. "I'll do my best," she whispered. "But Syd, be prepared for anything."

Lovely.

I watched Mom leave for the diplomatic clash between witch and vampire as Piotr appeared at my side, though he knew better than to touch me, at least.

"This way." He motioned for me to precede him, but I wasn't going anywhere with him. Not alone, anyway.

"Coven Leader." Sebastian bowed on my other side, gaze locked on his rival. "Allow me to escort you to your chamber."

I took his offered arm with a little curtsy, unable to help myself considering how he was dressed, though from the smile that broke for a moment, I felt certain I looked foolish doing it.

Sunny's face was stoic, Uncle Frank's equally so as they fell in behind us, cutting Piotr off while Charlotte, now mostly human, clung to my free hand, head whipping around as she whined under her breath.

"Thanks for the heads up," I whispered to Sebastian as we exited the throne room.

"I swear I had no idea." There was enough tension in his voice I knew he was telling the truth. "I only heard of this moments before you were kidnapped and have been working to free you since last night."

"You could have told me it was Batsheva." Yeah, I was grumpy.

"I would have, had I known the clan changed hands," he said. "It appears I'm not as trusted as I once was." Sadness. No, I would not feel sorry for him. "Though I must admit I'm surprised she was able to defeat Yvette in combat."

I wasn't. The Hayle family didn't have the market on horseshoes cornered, it seemed.

Two long corridors later, more stone, more tall, thin windows, more black carpet, and Sebastian closed the door on a chamber flanked by two of Pannera's vampires, cutting them off and leaving us alone.

Charlotte's face morphed back to human, though her eyes still held the wolf as she began a systematic snuffling around every corner and piece of furniture in what looked like a sitting room, vaulted fireplace black from centuries of flame. I watched her with worry while Sunny stepped forward and hugged me.

"Oh, Syd," she whispered. "What a mess. I'm so sorry."

"You're sorry." I hugged her back. "I ruined your shower."

She laughed and pushed me away, only to kiss my cheek with her cool lips. "Plenty of time for that," she whispered in my ear.

"Tell me you won't let this ruin the wedding." Why did the idea of that make me fret so much?

"Silly," Uncle Frank hugged me too. "Nothing could stop our wedding. Okay?"

Okay. I turned from him to face Sebastian who watched me with a mix of concern and amusement.

"Life is ever interesting with you as a companion," he said.

"Not my fault," I grumbled. "Speaking of which, I'm done now. Mom has them distracted and I'd like to go home. So if you all would just give me a hand, we'll cut out of this funhouse and let the politicians do their thing."

Sebastian's hesitation didn't warm my heart any. "It's not so simple," he said.

"Um, yeah, it is." I didn't want to be angry with him. Or throw a fit. Or destroy this centuries-old castle because of my temper. But, well. Things happened.

But even Sunny sighed, sinking into a chair probably as old as she was. "They will simply pursue you," she said. "And order us to bring you back."

"Which you wouldn't do." The look on Uncle Frank's face wasn't boosting my optimism, either.

"We wouldn't have a choice, demon girl." Sebastian turned from me to pace. Maybe I'd picked up the bad habit from him. Or maybe it was just the only solution when the mind was churning and the body couldn't help but respond. "As our Queen, Pannera's orders are tied to our blood. We have no say in the matter."

"Magic?" I joined Sunny who slid over to make room for me, despite the fact there were lots of low couches and divans and other things to sit on. I just didn't feel like being alone at the moment and when she put her arm around me I knew she was happy to oblige. "Compulsion?"

Sunny nodded, eyes sad. "It's the way of our people," she said. "How the clans keep order."

Though a convenient way to run things, the idea of no free will gave me the creepies.

"We need to trust the process." Sebastian came to a halt as though a decision solidified in his mind. "Your mother will help my Queen see reason."

"And if she doesn't?" I stood abruptly, needing space suddenly as much as I'd needed comfort. "You'll let your Queen strip me?" If she could.

Sebastian didn't say anything while the swish of fabric told me Sunny was also on her feet.

"Our Queen is as power hungry as she ever was," she snapped, temper crackling in her voice.

Sebastian spun on her. "You don't know her as I do."

"I know her better," Sunny said. "From the other side of the fight. From Yvette's side. Remember?" He turned from her as Uncle Frank reached out, maybe to silence Sunny, maybe to back her up, but she pulled free of his grip and continued her assault on Sebastian. "You would never listen, didn't want to know your precious Pannera was, and is, every bit as much a monster as Yvette."

"You were raised by the darkest of clans," he said, shoulders down, hands on the back of a chair, voice quiet. "What do you know of her honor?"

Sunny laughed, humorless, her beautiful face twisted with scorn. "This has nothing to do with honor, Sebastian. Only power." She pointed at me, but didn't look at me. "The power Syd holds inside her. Ambition, the need to rule everything. Where is the honor, I ask you?"

"Better her than Batsheva." Sebastian's hands tightened on the carved back of a chair.

"Better Syd, I say," Uncle Frank said.

The sharp crack of breaking wood made us all jump. Sebastian straightened, two chunks of elaborately carved flowers falling to his feet as the chair sagged to the side, broken.

"You think Pannera has the best interest of you and your clan at heart," Sunny said. "But you have no idea the hold she has over you, the lies she's made you believe. Nor have you seen the things I've witnessed, the atrocities she's ordered and participated in. Because you refuse to accept."

"I thought we were your clan now, Teresa." Sebastian turned to face her, fire brewing in his eyes. I'd heard her called that before. Nicholas used the name Teresa. But wait, Nicholas called her something else, a long time ago, the night I lost my demon. Sonja?

How many identities did my friend have?

Sunny couldn't know what I was thinking, shrugging as she looked away from Sebastian. Sighed. "At times like this," she said, "I feel clanless, my leader."

Neither of them spoke and the longer the silence went on, the more my heart broke until I had to shatter their horrible silence and the implications of it.

"I'll stay put." I stepped between them, taking their hands in mine, connecting them through me and the vampire inside me. "But I won't let them harm me or the one I carry."

"Will she go?" Sebastian's tension hummed through him and into me.

"No," I said. "She's made it very clear she won't tolerate either Queen. Nor anyone who considers her property."

The essence I held grasped a hold of me and shunted me aside, sending sparks of white power to both of them. Sunny's eyes widened as she spoke through me again. They may not have realized she'd done so before, but with full contact it was pretty clear who was addressing them.

"Forgive me, Sebastian DeWinter," she told him. "But I am grateful to you, for in your body I began to heal." She shuddered. "When your clan devoured me from the form of Cesard, my insanity grew worse. Being broken like that almost destroyed me."

"Which is why you controlled me." Sebastian nodded slowly, sadly. "I understand."

"No," she said. "You do not. Not really. I will never

allow myself to be divided again. Sydlynn spoke correctly—neither of your so-called Queens is worthy of me. I've chosen my home with the one heart who healed me simply by the kindness in her and the strength of her spirit." Wow. Blushing. "Sydlynn has returned my wholeness, but she has also reawakened my purpose. And I will not be swayed. If anyone tries, I will ensure my assimilation destroys them utterly."

Sunny squeezed my hand. "And what is your purpose?"

"To assist Sydlynn to evolve," she said. "And become of the Undying. A maji."

Chapter Ten

Kind of miffed. I hadn't been spreading that particular fate of mine around and here was the vampire side of me spilling it willy-nilly. Okay, not so nilly. But willy? Yup, yup.

At least from the startled look on my undead friend's faces the revelation was satisfactorily shocking. Enough to convince Sebastian to have my back?

From the sounds of it, he didn't really have a choice.

Sunny's flawless face looked so sad I hugged her, letting Sebastian go, breaking the bond as my vampire retreated again and let me take the reins.

"Syd," she whispered. "Oh, Syd."

No crying. Damn her and her sweet sympathy. I was so over it.

Yeah, right.

"Such a burden to carry alone." Sunny wiped at a

crystal tear on her cheek, clearly not as concerned about the whole weepy thing as I was, making it harder for me to keep the grip sadness had over my throat from forcing me to sob.

"I wish it mattered." Sebastian's shoulders rolled forward and for the first time since I'd met him, he looked defeated. "We all know, if Pannera orders us, we'll be forced to participate when Syd is stripped of the vampire essence."

"No," Sunny said, suddenly grim, arm around my waist while Uncle Frank came to stand behind me. "I will risk everything for the young woman who has done the same for me." She glared, the guilt trip she tossed at him so tangible I could almost breathe it in. "For all of us."

"I'm with my family," Uncle Frank growled. "My real family. Sunshine. Syd. This vampire clan thing can go to hell."

"You will be killed." Sebastian's tone didn't change, remaining quiet, calm. "At the very least stripped and banished from your blood clan. Left empty, powerless."

"Not if I have anything to say about it." I tapped one foot impatiently on the floor. Though I knew he was battling his loyalties, I'd saved his damned life. And no way was I letting anyone hurt Sunny and Uncle Frank.

Or Sebastian himself for that matter.

"Okay, tell me how this works," I said. "Like covens and the High Council, right? So you," I jabbed a finger at

Sebastian, "are like me and she," I flicked toward the door, meaning Pannera, "is like Mom?"

He nodded slowly. "Yes, in a way. But it's a much deeper attachment. She is the mother, literally, of all of us. Through her blood we were made. I carry it, and because of that, when I make a vampire, her control comes before mine."

Again with the all or nothing. Hmmm. I wondered if the coven would even consider it?

Yeah, not.

"I care for you deeply," he said. "My feelings will never be in question. And I owe you my soul. But you're asking me to betray my family."

Oh boy. All the anger slid out of me as I crossed to him and hugged him. His arms lifted, pulled me close, the subtle scent of roses just enough to tickle my nose.

"I understand," I said. "Family is everything."

He looked down at me in silence. Nodded. Stepped away, though his hand lingered in mine a moment before he released me.

"I guess we'll just have to wait and see what happens." And hope I wouldn't have to do something drastic to the people I cared about. It would break my heart to have to kill Sebastian.

"I'm going to check in with my old clan." Sunny's gown rustled as she turned. "Find out what really happened to Yvette. If there is something we can use against Batsheva."

I nodded. She had to be the key to this. As always.

"I'm with you." Uncle Frank turned and motioned to Sebastian. "Coming with us?"

"Not quite yet," he said. "Sydlynn, a moment?"

Wasn't like he was going to attack me or anything. Though from the worried look on Uncle Frank's face he wasn't so sure.

Charlotte completed her round of the room, now opening the door on the far wall, sliding through. I caught sight of a giant four-poster bed on the other side.

"Pannera saved my life too, once." Sebastian leaned on the back of a sofa, hands crossed before him, eyes on the carpet as his mind went to memory.

"You don't owe me an explanation." Yes, I was curious, of course I was. But I didn't want to push him when I had my own hide to worry about.

"I want you to understand," he said. Turned and sat on the settee before patting the cushion beside him in invitation. Why did the look in his eyes as he did so make me blush? Shunting aside the totally inappropriate thoughts racing through my head, reminding my libido this was a serious conversation and naughty thoughts about his deliciousness had no place, I perched next to him, hands fisted in my lap so they wouldn't shake.

He was so freaking yummy.

"When Nicholas turned, he came to me at once and

attacked me." Sebastian shifted forward, one arm around the back of the sofa, leaning in as he spoke. No way was he hitting on me or anything. But wow, did it make it hard to concentrate when his face was so close to mine, chiseled jaw begging to be stroked, silken hair falling over his forehead. "I was dying, would have died, if Pannera hadn't rescued me. Turned me into one of hers." His power slid over me softly. "I owe her everything. Not just my life. But my eternal loyalty. And no, it's not just the pull of my blood, Sydlynn. It's true family." His eyes pleaded with me as he reached out and slid his fingertips over my cheek, tucking a stray strand behind my ear. "I should have come to my Queen when the essence claimed my soul." She hissed inside me, cracking the spell he seemed to hold over my hormones, but only for a moment. "But I was afraid. This is all my fault." He sat back then, sighing from lungs which didn't need air. Old habits never died, I supposed.

Time for a wakeup. "This isn't your fault," I said. "Or mine. It's Batsheva's and Ameline's. And the damned maji who made you in the first place."

"I swear I will do everything in my power to keep you safe." He leaned in again, the weaving of his magic drawing me toward him as if he'd never pulled away. "I will convince my Queen. Somehow. But please, believe me. I had no idea this was coming." He shook his head, dark hair swaying, beckoning, tempting. "There was a time she and I were close." I didn't want to know how close as jealousy jabbed me, though I could guess from the old longing in his voice. "But no longer. When I chose to make a home for myself and my blood clan in the New World, she became cold, though geographical distance means nothing to us."

There was much more to this story than he was telling, but I didn't care. I just wanted him to keep talking and never stop.

"It's been worse between us since you freed me from the essence. I fear she will never forgive me for allowing such power to slip through her fingers." So he knew she wasn't perfect. Okay then. "But we have enough history, I think I can sway her."

"We'll see." I couldn't help myself, reaching out to take his hand, breathing in the scent of roses his clothing carried. "This has to end well."

"Why is that?" His lips twisted into the sexiest smile I'd ever seen.

"I'm immortal," I said. "No way am I spending eternity on my own. I'm going to need friends," I licked my lips, remembering our only kiss, the cool but delightful feeling of his mouth when he rewarded me in the cave after his release, "to spend it with."

Sebastian's eyes narrowed, heavy lidded, smile spreading as he bent closer. So close, too close, too far.

Damn it.

"Oh, how you tempt me, demon girl," he whispered.

"I'm not a girl anymore," I whispered back.

And I'm positive, absolutely positive, had Charlotte not chose that moment to walk through the bedroom door, I would have found out what kissing Sebastian could really be like.

Chapter Eleven

Sitting and waiting had never been one of my strengths, but after Sebastian rose abruptly at the interruption and left rather quickly, I didn't have much say in the matter.

Charlotte calmed enough she was back to mostly normal, though I knew her present state would change at the barest hint of a threat. It couldn't be easy for her, surrounded by her enemies, knowing my life was in danger, and I almost wished Anastasia hadn't brought her, no matter the insane demands I'm sure Charlotte made.

And though my usual reaction to being trapped and frustrated because my fate was being decided for me would be to pace or throw things or storm my way into more trouble, I found myself reclining on a divan, looking out at the silent mountains, lost in thought.

Did my demon and Shaylee, not to mention my

family magic, have that much of a restless influence on me? I certainly felt calm, almost relaxed, and had to blame—or thank—my vampire for my present emotional repose.

Though, of course, instead of trying to work my way through a plan of escape just in case I needed it, my mind went to love.

Not in a dreamy-steamy embarrassing kind of way. More of a pensive, what to do swirling softly around and around. I'd written love off because I just couldn't stand the thought of losing someone I cared about to old age while I remained young. But Sebastian, or someone like him… that was another option all together. It certainly opened up some interesting possibilities.

You must be cautious, my vampire sent. *While he cares for you, it is true, he is still her creature.*

Spoil sport. *I don't know,* I sent back. *I think, in the end, he'll back me if push comes to shove.*

Delusion does not become you, she sent.

It's not like it matters anyway. I picked at the fabric of the divan, the tapestry of woven colors making me dizzy. *If they do decide against us, we'll just give the Queens the old heave-ho and deal with it later.*

Again, delusion. She sighed. *You seem to be working under a flawed premise I've meant to speak with you about for quite some time.*

Sorry? Where was the flaw exactly? *It's not like they can really hurt me or anything. I'm immortal.*

Immortal, yes, she sent. *But not invincible.*

Gulp. *Explain?*

Immortality means you will live forever, and never grow old, she sent. *As long as nothing happens to you.*

That sounded rather final for something I was given the impression would go on and on forever. Why was this the first time I was hearing this information?

You can die, Sydlynn, she wrapped up her happy message. *I'm just not sure how much it will take to kill you.*

Didn't really want to find out. *It would have been nice to know this a while ago*, I sent.

She shrugged inside my mind. *I assumed you knew.*

Way to make me feel like a total moron.

Holy. Fear rose, bubbled, burst, choked me, drove me to my feet to pace. Charlotte startled, coming to me, but I waved her off, fighting the rush of panic this new bit of news rustled up.

This changed my perspective. On everything. My memory went to the beach, to surfing, the wave.

I could have drowned.

The basement of the Brotherhood house, the scent of gasoline, the pressure of sorcery holding me down.

I would have burned to death.

Holy.

Crap.

I spun as Charlotte snarled, eyes going to the window,

the brightening of the sky. But she wasn't focused on the newborn morning. Instead, she darted toward the bedroom door and flew inside, emerging a moment later with a small, shivering, silver-haired cherub in tow.

Demetrius smiled at me, blue eyes full of innocence as she dumped him on the floor at my feet.

"Sydlynn," he said. "I'm so happy to see you again."

Chapter Twelve

Charlotte looked ready for murder. Chances were she just needed someone to take out her nervous energy on. I was shocked she hadn't killed him already, to be totally honest about it. As she glared down at him he continued to smile at me, sweet face as creepy as ever, especially knowing what madness lurked behind his gentle eyes.

"Forgive me," he said, shuffling forward on his hands and knees to bend over and press his forehead to the top of my foot. "I told you the truth when we last met, I swear it." He looked up, a wide smile showing his perfect, even, white teeth, the scar marring his right cheek barely visible now he was human again and not in the demon form he'd been forced into. "You have an ally in Batsheva's clan."

"You let them drug me again." I stepped away from him, not wanting him to touch me. Charlotte took my disgust as permission to reach for him and jerk him to his feet, almost suspended from her hand as she hoisted him away from me.

"I had no choice." His words squeaked out past her grip on his throat. Probably not the best handle. I waved at her and, with a look of absolute disappointment, she let him go. He coughed a few times, still smiling. "But I knew you were stronger this time, gave them a weaker dose so some of your magic would remain."

Grumble, mumble. "What is it?" I shuddered inside at the emptiness he reminded me of.

"Powdered crystal," he said with a broad wink. "My own recipe. Gets into every cell, blocks off what it can't siphon." He hugged himself, rocking back and forth in clear delight. "Works very well, yes?"

Still crazy. Cracked to the core. "You're not seriously asking me to admire your handiwork?"

Demetrius dropped his arms, the hurt on his face making him look vulnerable.

"It only reached your surface magicks," he said. "They thought it would take care of you completely. But I was careful."

Well, at least I had the vampire. She grunted agreement. So maybe I should cut him a little slack.

"I'd say thanks," I said, "but I'm still in this mess. No offense."

He reached for me before Charlotte could get another

chokehold on him, but he just stroked my bare arm before backing off, smile returning.

"It's good, it's very good." He did a little hopping dance. "It's all you need to do the deed."

"What deed?" Crackpot had a plan?

"Why kill the old witch, of course, of course." He laughed out loud, insanity showing behind the veneer of kindness in his vivid, child-like eyes. "You must kill Batsheva."

Hmm. Good plan. And already on the menu.

"You can't." Charlotte's voice growled with the undercurrent of her wolf.

"She must." Dominic hissed back, baring his teeth as if he were the feral one.

She ignored him, faced me. "If you kill Batsheva, one of two things will happen." She held up one hand, ticking off a raised finger. "Doing so with any of your magicks, even your vampire power, in an unprovoked attack means a death sentence."

Not on the roster now I knew dying was a possibility again. "And two?"

"Even if you convince her to strike first, you'll have to use your vampire magic to make the battle valid. Which means draining her of power." She paused. "And blood."

Ickle to the power of infinity.

"I guess I can do that," I said. "If it's my only

option." Syrupy blood, hot from the kill—

Gag.

"You don't understand," Charlotte said. "Doing so means you will be the new Queen."

Oh. Not so good an option.

"So, you're telling me, it's basically a no-win here." I turned away from both of them as Charlotte's shoulders slumped. There had to be other choices.

Had to be.

"How did Batsheva defeat Yvette?" I turned as Charlotte spoke to find her shaking Demetrius by a strangle hold. Only his arm, this time. Even she knew holding him by the throat meant no answers to her questions, no matter how angry she felt. Especially because of how angry she felt.

Demetrius tried to free himself, whining like a puppy until she released him. He scrambled back from her, rubbing his arm.

"She has her ways," I said even as Charlotte chewed her bottom lip.

"I can't believe it," she said. "No one crossed Yvette Wilhelm. Even Odette was afraid of her." The vampire Queen would have to have been very powerful to shake someone as arrogant as Odette Dumont.

"And you know this how?" My wereguard shrugged, eyes flickering from wolf and back again.

"Let's just say my pack had run-ins with both vampire

clans," Charlotte said. "I was born and raised in Ukraine, but we had many dealings with covens and blood clans all over Europe thanks to Odette and her meddling with politics on the continent."

Why wasn't I surprised a crafty old witch like the deceased Dumont sister didn't cut her ties to the homeland when she brought her coven to the U.S.?

"How did Batsheva beat Yvette if Charlotte is right?" I returned my focus to Demetrius in time to catch him sticking his tongue out at my bodywere before he answered.

"She won the same way she does everything," he said. "Cheater."

"How?" I put myself between them, knowing Charlotte would just demand when it seemed Demetrius required my trust.

He bobbed his head, smile back. "She saved me," he said. "Because she needed me." From the trial. He would most likely have been put to death for his involvement in the High Council takeover and subsequent law-shattering behavior Batsheva implemented to destroy my mother and my family. "Took me here with her, when she begged the Queen to turn her. Offered her your essence." A way in. Just like Batsheva to worm herself into a place of power. As horrible as she was, she had a knack for getting what she wanted.

"The young one came too," he went on. "And horse-face."

Celeste I knew about. But the young one? "Ameline?" Of course. She had to have been part of it. How else would she have had access to Piotr and Yvette's vampires?

He hissed, but not at me. "Her," he said. "Both of them, offering the Queen a different plan for you. But neither was going to give you up, oh no." He cackled, wrung his hands. "Ameline lost, Batsheva won, Queen Yvette turned her personally." Demetrius stressed the word like it was very important. "The moment she did, Batsheva went to work. Celeste first. Then undermining, undercutting, talking and bribing on and on."

Again, typical Batsheva. "And Ameline?" If I could somehow manage to get my hands on her too, a big number of my dangling issues could be wiped out forever.

Leaving room for all the others. Shrug.

"Gone," he moaned, dashing my hopes. "Thick as two could be, yes, until Yvette chose and then the girl was no longer welcome."

Damn. Oh well.

"Then Batsheva, she was ready, had enough support," Demetrius said. "But not real support, bought, connived, stolen."

"Stolen?" I found myself frowning at the word. "What do you mean?"

"She had help." He pressed one finger to the side of his nose and winked, a demented fallen angel with a secret to share. "Big help, but the Queen, she didn't know it. No one knew it. Only me. Me. Because I brought the help to her so long ago."

He leaned close, looked at Charlotte like she wasn't worthy of knowing what he was about to tell me before his glistening blue eyes met mine again.

"I was the one who introduced her to the Brotherhood," he said.

Chapter Thirteen

In the moment it took me to understand just how deep Batsheva's evil ran, Demetrius plowed ahead as if he hadn't just dropped a magical nuke in my lap.

"I helped her make a crystal of her very own." He shook his head, tsking. "Foolish. She used it in secret to drain Yvette's magic while they fought." Charlotte rumbled her unhappiness. Not that the vampire Queen was betrayed, I didn't think, but more so out of her inherent sense of fair play. "Batsheva defeated her, easy peasy lemon squeezy, then drained her dry. Slurp."

Bile was the worst taste ever. I just wished I had control over its rise.

"Her crystal?" If I could get my hands on it... but no. Each one was keyed to the user. So no help there. But if I could somehow have mine brought to me, a whole bunch of new possibilities were available. That was, if it could break through the block from the powder. Though I had reason to believe that might be the case. After all, it allowed me access to my magic when I'd been magically smothered by the Brotherhood's sorcerous shields.

Demetrius giggled on the edge of hysteria, pointing at me. "No good to her as a blood sucker anymore," he said. "You breathed it in."

I could have done without that much information. Knowing something Batsheva used was inside me, devouring and blocking my power, made me want to turn my skin inside out and have a very, very hot shower.

"And the familial clan?" Charlotte prodded him. "They just accepted Batsheva?"

"Coerced," he nodded, sadness pulling at his scar, a weepy cherub fallen too far for redemption. "So unhappy. But what could they do?"

Charlotte's hands shook as she clenched them into fists at her sides. "Disgusting."

"You just described Batsheva," I said. "And Celeste."

"That one." Demetrius was suddenly a snapping animal full of venom and hate. "That one will die slowly and painfully and I will laugh, ho ho."

Creepy. But I just so happened to agree with the sentiment and, considering the ending my demon had planned for the woman, I didn't really have the right to judge.

"Demetrius, why the Brotherhood?" Not good at all.

"What do they get out of this?"

"Power," he said. "Control. Of course."

Of course. Ding ding, Syd. If they owned Batsheva, it meant they now owned one of the two most powerful blood clans in the world. And knowing the new vampire Queen Batsheva's ambitions, she'd soon be the only leader with control over the majority of the vampire nation.

Had to hand it to her. No matter how many times she tried and failed, she wasn't a quitter.

I had so many questions, but it turned out they had to wait. The sun had fully risen at last and as someone knocked on the sitting room door, Demetrius dashed for the bedroom and out of sight.

"Let him go," I said to Charlotte as she turned to go after him. "He'll be back."

I didn't argue with her when she gestured for me to stay put when she went to answer the knock. A tall, broad shouldered man with a coarse mop of dark hair and empty brown eyes towered over my bodywere, ignoring her after a quick sneer of disgust before fixing his ugliness on me.

"You will remain," he grunted in a heavy accent sounding Austrian or German. Not like my German class helped much, but at least I recognized the harshness. With that he spun and slammed the door behind him.

Rude. But then again, I felt a little sleepy, like the sun

shining in on me, the touch of a beam's heat driving my eyes to close—

Stop that. I jerked awake, annoyed to find I'd almost fallen asleep standing up.

Sorry, my vampire sent. *I've never had this much control before. And I usually nap on and off during the day while the others keep you occupied.*

No time to process that information, not at the sound of shouting outside my door and the dull thud of something or someone striking the heavy wood hard enough to crack it down the middle. The portal swung open, the big guard falling backward as Mom casually shoved him aside with a wall of magic and entered my prison like she owned the whole castle.

I resisted running to hug her, only because she wasn't alone. Margaret Applegate tromped in behind her, casting an annoyed look at the guard who slowly pulled himself to his feet.

"Manners," she snapped. "Find some. Now get out."

He did as he was told, the door closing though a jagged crack ran the width of it, vibrating along the break as it thudded closed.

I grinned at Mom. "That had to hurt."

"I certainly hope so." She embraced me, no concern for appearances, so I hugged her back and tried not to let my tears get the better of me. I'd always accused her of being a supernatural faucet, but I was at least as bad.

I was so happy to see her.

Margaret didn't share our emotion. She swung one fist against her leg over and over, black robe gaping open, tweed suit and pantyhose showing through. The hole in her right stocking must have caused her no end of irritation, the run reaching the top of her very sensible shoes.

Still, she was a witch and, so far, seemed to be on our side. So why was she looking at me like I was something unpleasant she had to take out to the trash?

"Well, my girlio, you've put me in a pickle of a spot."

She called me what? "Coven leader." Oops. I really, really didn't mean to be so cold in correcting her. But years spent watching Mom manage our family and those who came against us kicked in out of habit.

Mom went rigid next to me. "Manners," she said in her most imperious tone. "Find some."

I'd never thought of my mother as having a temper. She always played things so cool. Yes, if she was pushed, she was a banshee from the deepest bowls of Scaryland, but normally she preached politics and diplomacy.

Which meant Margaret was already pissing her off and this was a last straw situation.

Good to know the older woman didn't have my back after all.

Margaret's eyes narrowed, but she nodded abruptly. "Coven leader," she said in a voice of blades. "Maybe you can tell me what I'm supposed to do about this mess you've dropped on my doorstep?"

Um, hello. "Excuse me," I snapped. "Where exactly in any of this did you decide I was at fault?"

Margaret's thumping fist came to a sudden stop. "I don't know how you Americans do things," she shot back, "but in my territory we abide by treaties and laws and don't butt into the business of other races." She snorted. "And we like it that way."

Oh, no she did *not*. "Right. So you'd rather ignore what's going on under your nose in favor of tra-la-laing along. Like them invading our territory to kidnap me. How nice."

Mom's face was white, pinched as though she was thinking what I said out loud, but forced to hold it in for fear of exploding or destroying diplomatic channels. That was just fine. I'd long decided she was happy having me perform as her action hero, doing her dirty work when she was unable to take steps. I'd add mouthpiece to my list of duties.

My pleasure.

"At least my territory is secure," she snapped back, magic cracking around her. "And not a continuing disaster crashing into an apocalypse."

Mom twitched, but I was faster. "I see." I crossed my arms over my chest and smiled at Mom, though my humor was nowhere to be found, thanks. "So I guess that means you don't want to know what your particular brand of governing has allowed to happen. In your territory."

Mom's eyes narrowed as Margaret spluttered.

"Whatever are you talking about?" I heard the girl at the end before Margaret caught herself. "Coven leader."

I filled them both in on what Demetrius told me while Mom nodded slowly and Margaret grew redder and redder in the face.

"Can you trust him, Syd?" Mom's question was calm, reasonable. But her eyes were troubled.

"Yes," I said, without a doubt. "Absolutely. He wants Batsheva dead, M—Council Leader. And he wants me to kill her."

"All this Brotherhood nonsense." Margaret dusted off the front of her robe as if doing so would erase what I just told her. "Nonsense."

Mom fixed her with that same cold stare. "Like it or not, we will be going to war," she said. "The Brotherhood will give us no choice. But we can either allow it to happen to us, or take matters into our own hands before it's too late."

"And Demetrius hates the Brotherhood more than Batsheva," I said. "So yes, Mom," I was okay with the word, screw Margaret Applegate, "I trust him."

The portly leader looked like she was ready to argue again, but when she finally exhaled a heavy breath, there was worry on her face. "I'll look into it," she said.

Would have to do. Time to change the subject to one near and dear anyway.

"Tell me I'm going home?" Mom's eyes gave me the information I needed before she opened her mouth.

"Not yet, I'm afraid," she said.

"Maybe never." Margaret sank to a chair, ankles crossed as she scowled at the carpet. "The Queens are both adamant and, frankly, I'm on their side in this." She met my gaze, not as openly hostile as she had been, but guarded nonetheless. "You do have vampire power. The source of their magic, if they are to be believed." I nodded. That much was true. "They have the right to it."

They don't, my vampire snapped.

"She begs to differ." It was hard not to sigh and stomp my foot in frustration.

"I can't have a race war in my territory." Margaret's hands clung together in her lap. "I won't have it, not over a witch who isn't even one of mine."

"You may not have a choice." Mom tapped her chin with one finger, the lines I'd started to notice on her face prominent as she frowned.

Of course. "This is the plan," I said. "The Brotherhood's goal. They don't care who wins, who they recruit."

Mom nodded, face smoothing out as she dropped her hand. "They just want a war."

Margaret looked quite horrified as it sunk in at last.

She pushed up, almost standing before falling back to her seat. "It's really happening," she said. At least she was admitting it to herself.

"It is," Mom said. "The Brotherhood isn't ready to move openly, but they've begun to undermine us. Stirring up trouble to deflect from what they are doing."

I reached for her hand and squeezed it as Margaret finally gained her feet, a little, round thundercloud.

"The hell they will," she said. Paused. "I'm almost done my term. So close, Miriam. And you had to bring this to me." Sighed. "Well, I'm not leader for nothing, am I?"

Mom's smile lit her blue eyes, the only ageless part of her. "I have every faith in you, Margaret."

"Hrumph." The older witch shook herself a little. "I suppose that means we need to find a way to save this daughter of yours."

"Yes, please," I said.

Margaret bobbed her head. "I'll alert my Enforcers," she said. "Time to dig out the weeds in my garden. And in the meantime, we'll work out some kind of solution. Hopefully one that doesn't start Armageddon." She rolled her eyes, offered a wee little smile. "You do realize how hard this is going to be? Damned vampires. Never met such a bunch ready to kill each other at the slightest provocation."

I grinned. "You haven't been to Demonicon," I said.

She shuddered. "No," she said. "And I have no wish to." Margaret had gone back to being someone I kind of liked. She may have been a bit hide-bound, but she was stepping up.

Couldn't ask for more than that.

"We'll do our best, sweetheart." Mom hugged me again.

"Let's just hope the solution we reach is one we can live with," Margaret said. "Though I don't think you're going to end up with everything you want."

There was a shocker.

Snort.

Chapter Fourteen

Margaret left us, presumably to talk with her Council, and even though she'd come around, I was still happy to have Mom alone for a little while.

She hugged me again, not letting go this time as she led me to a settee and drew me down beside her. The segment of her magic tied to vampire power, thanks to Batsheva herself no less, connected with mine and, in that moment, the world opened up again.

Beginning with a very angry tirade from Gram.

When I get my hands on that tart of a bitch with a capital 'B'—

She wasn't alone.

—can't say out of trouble for ten minutes. That was Sassafras, piggybacking into our conversation. I didn't mind. Not even a little.

Enough, you two. Mom stroked my hair while I leaned

against her and just let her be my mother. *Syd's been through a lot in the last few hours. And none of this is her fault.*

Of course it isn't, Gram snapped.

What's the hold up? Sassafras's amber magic snaked inside me. The moment it did, I felt his panic. *I thought you were just out cold*, his mind's voice fell to a whisper. *Syd. What happened?*

A quick recounting of the story since I was kidnapped followed. Mom must have been blocking out the pair of them because they reacted to each revelation with shock and anger.

Tell me you've ripped out Batsheva's black heart and force-fed it to her? Gram shared a helpful image.

Mom sighed inside my mind. *Mother*, she sent. Chided, actually. Though I firmly agreed with Gram's desire to wrench the evil woman's life away in as painful and humiliating a fashion as I could muster. *You're not helping.*

This is ridiculous. Sassafras actually spluttered. *They have no right. Not only is Syd outside their territory in the first place, possession is nine-tenths of the law.*

He was watching too many procedural cop shows again.

Or was he?

You're correct, Mom said. *And were this my territory, I would deal with the two vampire Queens with a very firm hand. But it isn't. And I can't.*

First things first, Sassy sent. *We have to find a way to free Syd's other powers. No offense to the vampire inside you, but you're on much firmer ground if you have personal backup.*

None taken, the vampire sent. *Might I intrude?*

Bless them, my family sat stunned a moment before Mom piped up.

Of course, she sent. *Your existence is as much at risk as Sydlynn's.*

Thank you for understanding, she sent. *Because I'm standing my ground. I will not be divided, nor join efforts with one of those... creatures.* Her disdain rang clear as a bell. *I will flee and live alone before I allow that to happen. But I would much prefer to stay right where I am. As for your suggestion, Sassafras, I have grown accustomed to the others who live with me and would very much like to have their support again.*

Nice to know everyone living in my body was getting along.

How did you free yourself when Demetrius used the powder on you last time? Mom. I guess I never told her.

Sebastian. I sat up abruptly. Stupid, stupid. I had him here, alone with me. Why didn't I have him repeat the performance? His power had "bitten" me, the spirit magic of vampires helping my body shed the influence of the powder. Hope faded a little. *I was dosed under orders*, I sent. *Which means he might not help me.*

Gloom settled over us. *All we can do is ask him*, Mom said.

Ask? Gram snarled. *Let me at him and he'll be begging to help. He thinks he's scared of that Queen of his? I'll show him scared.*

There was no way I could hold in my laughter. *I love you, Gram.*

She grunted, but her mental touch softened. *I feel useless*, she finally sent.

So do I. Sassafras's demon power felt different without my own, but his worry came through anyway.

We all do, Mom sent. *But we've faced hardship before. And we've always survived it. I have faith this will resolve itself.*

Good thing someone did.

Patience, the vampire sent. *There is a time for action but there is also a time for learning, understanding. We must wait and see what unfolds through diplomatic channels. Perhaps there will be a way to turn whatever ruling comes out of it to our advantage.*

Okay, I'd buy that. *As long as it doesn't involve me dying*, I sent, *or becoming a real vampire, it's all good.*

She shuddered, my body suddenly covered in goosebumps. *Agreed*, she sent. *I like you just the way you are.*

So do I. Gram's gruff words were followed by a mental hug and wet smack. *Keep us posted.*

Sassafras's farewell feeling was much less optimistic, but included a hug of his own before he was gone.

"Time for me to do some research." Mom rose from her seat. "I'm not up on European law, or their treaties. I felt out of the loop in negotiations last night."

I didn't want her to go, but knew she had to. "Need some help?"

She smiled, stroked my cheek. "You get some rest," she said, kissing me softly in the same place her fingers had touched. "I'll see you shortly."

I had every intention of doing as she told me. But I just couldn't seem to settle. Food arrived twice through that endless day while I paced and napped and paced some more, Charlotte kindly steering clear.

Unable to relax enough to allow a full sleep, I went exploring in my room as the shadows started to lengthen, the sun finding its way to the horizon. An antique shower was a welcome sight, a happy surprise to find in an old castle, but I supposed even vampires appreciated more modern amenities than heating water with fire. I scrubbed down under the fall of hot water, emerging to a large terry robe and a giant closet full of dresses.

Charlotte had already sniffed her way through it and deemed it safe for me to enter. Like there was some fabric monster in there ready to eat me. Though from the look of some of the gowns, it was a distinct possibility. I glanced at my sundress laid out over the back of a chair, now a wrinkled, dirty mess and sighed. At least the clothes in this closet weren't so avant-garde as to be unrecognizable as attire. I still puzzled over some of the pieces I'd come across in my Demonicon selection and felt sure I'd never find out what they were for.

Or want to.

Ball gowns at least were familiar, though I did spot a few riding outfits, complete with tall leather boots and velvet jackets, lacy blouses spilling their guts over the front of sheer white shirts.

No way was I doing skin-tight pants in this company. So a dress it was. My eyes went immediately to the blue selection, my best and favorite color. At least if I was going to put on a show when they called me to my doom I could look my best.

And who knew Charlotte had a way with hair and makeup? When she caught me dabbing on some mascara and a bit of gloss, my wet hair hanging over my bare shoulder, she rolled her eyes and took me firmly in hand.

Firmly.

By the time she was done, I felt like I was going to prom. Only this time, instead of the caked-on perfection Erica insisted I wear, the accenting colors my wereguard chose were subtle, enhancing my appearance rather than changing it. My dark hair, no pile of curls for me, spun in ringlets from a low ponytail tucked to one side, strings of crystals woven through to catch the light. The cut of the heavy dress left a little more of my chest exposed than I liked and Charlotte was every bit as vicious with the ties on the corset as I expected, but I had to admit the end result was startling.

I told you, the vampire inside me said. *They need spirit power to enhance their beauty. You already have it.*

Well now. Blushing.

I stepped out of the bedroom and into the sitting room as the sun set behind the mountains, plunging the room into darkness. Skirt swishing over my heels, I turned to Charlotte only to feel the compression of air preceding a vampire teleport. I spun back just in time to catch Batsheva's errand boy, Piotr, as he appeared, latching onto my arm and dragging me away with him.

I was stunned and drugged last time he tried it. Not so this time. The moment he teleported us away, I let the vampire out. She sliced through his defenses with knife cuts of spirit power, staggering him as her magic took control of the teleport and brought us to a halt.

You were expecting this? She sounded approving.

We both were. I fretted a moment over Charlotte. She had to be losing her little werewolf mind back in my room, but she wasn't my focus. Couldn't be. *What now?* I already knew.

My vampire was kind enough to offer options. *We can go back*, she sent. *Or we can deliver a message.*

I liked how she thought very, very much.

After a moment of jerking free memories from Piotr's nasty little brain, my vampire found the location she went looking for and we were off again. We emerged in a massive chamber of stone and wood, a fire roaring in a giant hearth, a crowd of exquisitely dressed vampires turning to face us with shock and fear while Batsheva rose to her feet, a scowl on her face, one that deepened as I dumped the unconscious Piotr to the carpet and gave him a firm kick in the ass.

"I accept your invitation," I said.

Celeste leaned in and whispered to her, but Batsheva shoved the vampire away, surging toward me with fury in her eyes.

And... madness. I'd always thought she was crazy, but in a brilliant and conniving kind of way. The level of nuts I saw in her at that moment was the first time I ever doubted my judgment.

Either she'd lost some of her mojo when she'd become a vampire or I'd given her way too much credit all along.

"Seize her." Batsheva's order sent that group of stunning undead toward me, though I saw them fighting her, faces twisting as though in pain.

A blast of magic sent them back. "I said I accept your invitation." I felt certain I could take them, but then again, neither my vampire nor I knew our limits without my alternate magicks as backup.

Damn it. At least I could put on a good show. *Sebastian*, I sent.

I'm here.

Batsheva kidnapped me again. I let him feel my rage in a sharp shot of power. *I'll be leaving shortly.*

Spirit magic jabbed, cutting me off.

"Your pet can't help you," Batsheva hissed, face twisting. No amount of vampire goodness could make her beautiful at that moment. "This is my castle. No one is permitted entry unless I allow it."

Vampire rules. They had more idiotic edicts than demons. I hated them so much.

"What do you want?" I know, I know. It was pretty obvious.

Batsheva bared her teeth, showing me the glittering points of her fangs. "Why, just to talk." She cackled a laugh, turning in a circle, stopping to eye me up and down, her smile fading to a vicious smirk while her fingers played with one of her curls. "Aren't you just sweet in your little outfit?" Hmm. Jealous much? "Though, you're nothing compared to me." Laughter again. She'd clearly lost her mind when she'd lost her life. "Tell me, Sydlynn—what do you think of my new look?" She spun to the left, waving her hands as three vampires scrambled out of the way so she could look at herself in a huge mirror. "You had no idea it was me, I'm so beautiful now."

"Impressive," I said. "Death becomes you."

She shot me a smile, a real smile. Was she that deluded?

What the hell was wrong with her?

"I am, I know." She turned to the side, ran her hands

over her thin waist once chunky. "And I'll be this beautiful forever."

"On the outside." It slipped out, I swear.

No more smile, just a look of venom so deadly I waited to keel over.

"Enough of your insolence," she snapped. "And enough of you and your precious little coven." Celeste hissed at her, but Batsheva ignored any attempt to silence her. "I will have your death and nothing will stop me."

Unhinged and undead. Not a good combination. I almost felt sorry for her while my mind whispered the question of how much of it had always been her and how much was the Brotherhood.

That was a very scary thought.

I spotted Demetrius, hovering behind the vampires, his blue eyes locking on mine for a moment before he hid again. Seeing him reminded me to prod her further. Maybe she'd become so unstable she'd implode.

Wishful thinking.

"How's Ameline these days?" As casual as asking about the weather. But it had the desired effect.

Batsheva spit like a pissed off cat as her skin glowed suddenly with power, fangs growing and retreating in a moment. "That girl has no sense. I offered her a perfectly good deal and what did she do?"

The other vampires backed away from her, fear and loathing on their faces as she tossed her hands up, lighting strikes of power lashing out around her. Nice to know they might not back her if they had the chance to take her down.

Wasn't counting on it.

"I couldn't begin to guess," I said.

"She ran off, chasing some stupid pipe dream." Batsheva jabbed one sharp index finger at me. "And, as usual, it's all your fault."

Mine?

"The Brotherhood offered her an excellent deal." Batsheva fanned herself, irritation growing.

Celeste's face morphed into rage for an instant before settling again, her eyes snapping fire at me. I guessed she had no idea that particular Brotherhood-loving feline was long out of the bag.

"Excellent!" Batsheva's eyes glittered from the affront. "Instead she's out there, stealing bits of magic like a common thief, thinking she's the next evolution. Whatever that means."

My.

Heart.

Stopped.

Beating.

"What?" I had just enough air to push that questioning word out of my vibrating body.

"Foolishness," Batsheva said while my heart stuttered back to life, though the anxiety in me didn't fade. "As if she could be anything more than she is now. As if demon power, vampire power, Sidhe power could help her find some kind of greater fate." Batsheva shook her head, anger gone, laughing softly as though the benevolent leader chastising an errant child. "She'll be disappointed and come back to me on her hands and knees." Vicious again. "And I'll crush her when she does."

I wasn't even really listening to Batsheva anymore. Not while I struggled with the truth, wanting to deny it, shut it off, find a way to unhear what I'd just heard.

None of this mattered anymore, not the vampires or the treaties or even my own fate.

Not while Ameline was out there trying to become maji.

CHAPTER FIFTEEN

Batsheva rambled for a while until even Celeste began to look embarrassed by her leader's behavior, all about her plans for dominance and what she was going to do to Pannera, to my mother, to Margaret, on and on in a spiraling downward vortex of cray-cray.

I watched Celeste carefully and realized very quickly the force of power had shifted between them. Though Batsheva came across as the leader, from the moments of hatred puncturing her calm, it was clear Celeste now held the reins, allowing the other woman to act as some kind of deranged figurehead. And though I wasn't sure why, just yet, Celeste must have had a plan. Possibly with the help of the Brotherhood.

Which meant she was now the more dangerous of the two.

Hard to take Batsheva seriously anymore as she paced

and snarled before cackling and twirling like a demented fairy tale princess in front of her mirror. Sad, actually. Depressing. As much as I was happy to see her go down, I wanted her to be aware of her fall. Her defeat now seemed like a mercy killing.

One good thing came out of it. Everything she babbled confirmed what Demetrius told me. So I knew I could trust him. Nice to know I hadn't lied to Mom and Margaret.

Whatever Batsheva's original plan for bringing me to her chamber, by the time she wound down, Piotr finally groaning awake at my feet, a heavy knock on the door broke up the festivities. Six bulky Enforcers entered, black cloaks sweeping around them as the lead, a hefty man with jowls to rival a bulldog, spoke in his British accent.

"The negotiations reconvene," he said. "Your presence is requested."

Way to save the day. Batsheva dimpled at him, though her blue eyes flashed with anger.

"Of course," she snarled. Glanced at me. Turned even paler than usual, quite a feat. Spun on Celeste. "We were supposed to kill her."

Celeste's scowl almost made me laugh as she grasped her leader's arm. "Time to go, my Queen."

"But we brought her here to kill her. Why is she alive?"

I almost commented, wondering why the Enforcers watching this particular farce unfold didn't comment, react, nothing. It was up to me. And I was so close, snark hovering on my lips. But I let it go, let them leave without further comment, two Enforcers coming to my side as their leader nodded to me.

"Miss Hayle," he said. "I'm Elliot Pearson. Margaret sent me for you. You're well?"

"A little bored," I said. "Thanks for the rescue." I followed him out into the corridor where Pender and two other of Mom's Enforcers waited.

"She's all yours," Elliot said. Winked at me. "You've got my vote, missy."

Flirt. I winked back. "Nice to hear it."

Pender bowed stiffly to his counterpart and waited until the others left, Elliot whistling to himself, before bending over me.

"Your mother was concerned," he said, voice strained. "I hope you're well?"

"Very well." A laugh bubbled inside me at the absurdity of my last hour or so. "I have to talk to Mom."

His face crumpled. "Not possible now," he said. "Margaret reconvened the talks only a short time ago, though they should break in a bit. Shall I escort you back to you quarters?"

The very place I wanted to be, trapped in my princess cave. "I guess so."

Lost in thought, trying to come up with a way to use Batsheva's madness against her, I didn't even consider the fact something else might be amiss until I found myself outside my door.

What was left of my door. It had already been damaged when Mom put on her little show of don't screw with Miriam Hayle. But now it lay scattered on the floor in large chunks and sharp splinters, claw marks gouged so deep in some of the pieces they almost reached all the way through.

Thought left me, terror gripping my throat in a chokehold as I ran through the gap and looked around at the devastation. Shattered furniture laid crushed and crumpled, fabric torn, the carpet ripped in strips. By claws.

Very sharp claws.

"Charlotte!" I raced to the bedroom where the overturned four-poster told me a story that only increased my fear for her. I spun to Pender who looked as shocked as I did. "Where is she?"

"I don't know." He turned and snapped his fingers and the two Enforcers with him dashed off. "We'll find her."

Panic. I reached for her, dove for my vampire. *Your kind hate werewolves*, I sent. *Can you track her through that?*

I don't hate them, she sent. *It's the young one's taint that drives them to such bias.*

Whatever. *Can you find her or not?*

Patience, Sydlynn, she sent. *I'm as worried as you are.* Pause, painful, slow, agonizing, wretched. *I've found her.*

Our minds flashed together, out of my body and to Charlotte—

Snarling, snapping, in pain, devoured by rage, an iron chain holding her down, icy cobbles under her feet, the open sky above while stone walls hold her in.

And the enemy. Cold, their scent of the grave and dust and death, surrounding her. Coming for her with their fangs, ready to drain her blood.

I jerked back to myself and reached for my vampire, trying to transport.

They're blocking her location from me. Even she sounded desperate. *I can see her, but I can't get a fix on where they are holding her.*

I didn't wait for her to finish, already running, out the door, Pender on my heels.

And into two bulky vampires who tried to stop me.

"Where is she?" My entire body vibrated with the need to hurt them both so much they would beg me to stop. Beg.

One of them shrugged with a little smile, but the other snarled at me.

"The foul creature attacked our kind," he said. "She waits in the courtyard for her execution."

I reached out with my magic, my vampire grasping

both of them by the throat and slamming them into the wall, jerking them off their feet until they writhed from the pressure, howling in outrage until I tightened my grip, squeezing their undead bodies while they cried out in pain.

"You will take me to her," I said, the ice cold fury of my vampire pulling me deep into her magic, "and if even a hair on her head has been harmed, I will kill you both."

CHAPTER SIXTEEN

It wasn't far to go to the courtyard I'd seen in my mind. Good for the pair of vampires I held firmly in my grip. Not so good for the crowd gathered around the panting, snapping, howling mess of my bodywere.

I emerged at a stomping pace through a half-open door into the chilly evening air, my breath escaping in a soft puff of white from my mouth as my heels clattered over the cobbled courtyard. The interior space was all stone just as the vision showed, tall windows high above blacked out, the clear sky sharply pinpointed with uncaring stars.

The two vampires in my grip went sliding forward and crashed into their fellows as my vampire power propelled them along, the hovering mob hissing and swiping at Charlotte, glimpses of her through their milling bodies showing me she'd transformed into her werewolf shape. They turned almost en masse to glare at me, spirit magic flashing in flames and lightning strikes around them.

Assholes. Charlotte crouched, clothing torn to shreds around her, tongue hanging from her furred snout as she hunched over scorch marks on her pelt. Still mostly human shaped though larger in size, back legs hinged like a wolf's, she represented the best of both races, tied into one very dangerous package.

If she'd been free, the vampires wouldn't have stood a chance. But chained and collared, tortured from a distance while her only focus was on finding and saving me, she was at a distinct disadvantage.

One I was about to correct.

They let me through, though I felt their animosity, none of them bending to help their fellows rise from where they'd fallen. Nice to know family meant so much to them. I ignored them as though they were of no consequence, though I snarled and let my vampire show her power to one who reached out to pull me back. The vampire retreated, ducking her head while she hissed at me.

Charlotte whined, low and deep, a painful sound as I came to stand next to her. I wished I could crouch and put my arms around her, comfort her, but no way was I showing weakness in front of this particular bunch. Not when the icy fury of my vampire still had a firm hold, fed by my own human rage.

The locked cuff around her neck released under my touch, spirit magic tearing apart the mechanism holding it in place. She clawed at it a moment until it fell free, clattering to the chilly stones, the sound echoing back at us from the surrounding walls. I reached for her cuffs when one of the vampires finally managed to stir enough guts to speak out.

"Stand aside," he snarled. I spun on the vampire who spoke as he continued, pretty-boy face ugly to me, no matter how polished undeath made him. "This abomination is sentenced to die."

"On whose authority?" I touched her cuffs, heard them fall away, felt her slide up beside me, pressing her furred body against my skirt.

"Vampire authority," he snapped back, looking around for support while the others nodded, power pulsing and fluttering.

"Just so you know," I said. "You have no idea who you're dealing with. Not really." *Are you ready to fight for her?* I reached for my vampire.

No spoken answer. But yes, yes indeed. She was so ready.

The pulse of magic she'd sent out in the throne room had scattered the approaching vampires, knocked a few down. I'd been impressed. But that had nothing on the sheets of lightning she now sent out, slamming full-force into the central mass of the hovering vampires, sending them back at such a speed thunder rolled through the quiet of the courtyard, the sound of splintering bone and cries of pain rumbling like an approaching storm.

"Just so you know," I said.

Naturally I was given a glare or two by Margaret as she and Mom, the two Queens flaring with rage behind them, hurried into the courtyard to survey the damage.

I reached down and helped Charlotte to her feet, wincing inwardly as her face shifted, hands shrinking, her human form taking over again. She stood shivering beside me at last, one arm over her exposed chest, head down, body covered in tiny burns, the remains of her torture session.

All of a sudden my vampire's attack just didn't seem like it was enough. And from the rush of her power flooding to the surface, she agreed with me.

I didn't get a chance at a second strike. Not with Margaret sizzling with magic, plump body blocking my way.

"What the bloody hell is going on out here?" She spun to survey the damage before refocusing on me. "Tell me this was self-defense."

"Absolutely," I said. "These undead," I wrinkled my nose though I caught the wince from Sebastian as he joined us, Sunny wide-eyed with a grinning Uncle Frank beside her, "dared to attack my bodywere. Mine." I pulled

Charlotte closer. "Under my protection."

Margaret heaved an angry sigh as Pannera drifted forward. "What is the meaning of this, Pannera?"

The vampire Queen caught my gaze and held it. "I surely don't know," she said.

"Batsheva." The name grated from between the portly Council Leader's clenched teeth.

"This thing attacked my people, from what I understand." Batsheva sniffed, turned away as though the sight of Charlotte offended her. "Punishment is death. Law. Vampire law."

"Like I said," I shot back. "Charlotte is under my protection."

"And mine," Mom said, stepping forward. "If she attacked your vampires," Mom didn't even bother to turn and address Batsheva directly, a total snub I would hug her for later, "it was because Syd's life was in danger. She is, after all, her protector. So tell me, Batsheva," Mom spun slowly at last, her very best cold, powerful, majestic face firmly in place, "was my daughter's life in danger?"

Batsheva had enough of a hold on her marbles to stay quiet.

"And yet," Pannera said, narrowed eyes locked on Charlotte, "the werewolf attacked vampires. What are we to do about the law?"

"Maybe if you people would stop kidnapping me," I snarled back, vampire rising, a challenge right there on the edge of my tongue, "she wouldn't have to defend me against you. Or defend herself for that matter."

Right back atcha.

Pannera's scowl deepened, but I didn't give her a chance to talk. Hell no, not while I was on a roll.

"I'll tell you one thing," I said, stepping forward into her space while her vampires hissed at me, "the next time one of you tries it, I'm not going to stop at broken bones. The offender will be dead for real. And there won't be any coming back from the kind of death I'll deliver, you better believe it."

Pannera didn't exactly back down. There was too much anger in her for that. But I guess I got my message across because she spun and refocused her attention on Batsheva. "I want to know why she was in your company, alone."

I snorted, actually enjoying the irritation Pannera showed at my amusement and the sudden defensiveness on Batsheva's face. More interesting, however, was the flare of anger and disgust from Celeste before she put a cap on it.

"You're just pissed she had access to the power and you didn't," I whispered to Pannera. Who twitched as if I'd poked her with a pin.

"Enough of this childishness." Margaret rubbed her face with both hands. "Vampires. A bunch of petty children with stupid rules and not a lick of sense among you."

Pannera backed off, though even as her face settled into calm, she allowed her power to touch the vampire inside me.

"Your pet may live," she said, much to the disappointed outcries of the gathered vampires, some of whom had recovered and regenerated enough to join us again. "But you are responsible for her, Sydlynn. And if she breaks our laws, it will be as though you have, too."

Oh, *hell* no.

"One more attack," she said with a small smile now mirrored by the hovering vampires, "and I'll kill her while you watch, before draining you dry."

Chapter Seventeen

The words, "You can try," bounced around in my head the whole walk back to my quarters. Charlotte remained glued to me, blonde hair falling over her face. I stopped near the doorway to the interior of the castle, the cold air pushing against my back and confronted Sebastian with a glare I was sure surprised him.

"Jacket," I snapped.

He slid it free, broad shoulders straining against his white shirt as he laid the velvet jacket around Charlotte's shoulders before bowing his head to me and backing away.

A little respect? Yeah, I'd take it, though I wondered what the show cost him.

I waited until we were behind the brand-new door a pair of human servants installed before turning on Charlotte and screaming at her.

Well, screaming was a bit of an exaggeration. Talking very loudly and with great emotion while my body shook so much I could barely catch my breath was more like it.

She took my anger and fear, finally uncurling from her hunch, Sebastian's jacket pulled tight around her. When I wound down, panting and pacing, she nodded slowly. Miserably.

"May I go clean up now?"

Seriously. "Just git." I waved at the bedroom door. "And the next time you decide to go after vampires in their territory, you'd better make sure they finish you off before I get my hands on you."

She flashed me a little smile. "Sounds familiar," she said. Hadn't she warned me of the same thing on the beach, not so long ago?

I grunted, but couldn't help smiling back. "Are you okay?"

Charlotte shuddered, a dog shedding water. "I will be," she said, ever so softly. "Thank you for rescuing me." Her eyes met mine, open, young. For the first time in a long time, I remembered she was my age, just a teenager doing an adult's job, giving a really good impression of hiding how scared she must have been most of the time. "Thanks to both of you."

My vampire sighed softly, a thin thread of white magic sliding out of me and stroking hair from Charlotte's cheek before retreating again. The weregirl turned silently and padded to the bedroom, softly closing the door behind her.

We were left alone for a long time, long enough Charlotte cleaned up and re-emerged, dressed in one of my riding get-ups, Sebastian's jacket over her arm. She looked much better herself, though a small, dark bruise on her right cheek told me she'd done wonders with hiding what happened behind her usual stoic attitude.

"We have to talk." I led her to a sofa, sat next to her. "You're not going to like it."

Charlotte just stared at me, blank face back. Um-hum.

"You can't do that again," I said. Felt like a broken record. "Charlotte, do you understand?"

She nodded. "I can't help it," she said. "And I'd repeat my actions in a heartbeat."

Oh boy. "They'll kill you next time," I said. "And they won't give me a chance to save you."

A moment of anxiety showed through her mask. "I can't," she said, a bit of puppy whine in her voice. "The *кодекс честі* won't let me."

The what?

She sighed and sat back, accent more noticeable than usual. "My people, our ways. The *кодекс честі*. It means debt. Honor debt." Her head swiveled slowly toward me, eyes sad. "It goes back to the days when we served the Czars. But it is the name we use for the bond we have to those we protect."

"Charlotte." I drew a deep breath so I wouldn't yell at her again. "You don't owe me anything."

"I do," she said. "My pack does. My father was to be your *охоронець*. Um... bodyguard. But he had no honor." Tears filled her eyes, tears she dashed away with great anger, the wolf flashing in her eyes for a moment before retreating again. "It was up to me to rebalance the pack's *сан*."

Even I could figure that one out. "Trust me," I said, "you've done more than enough to bring honor to your pack." I hesitated, only because she'd already been through so much and I knew what she was going to say to my next suggestion. No, what she was going to do. But I had to try. "I think it's time we severed the bond."

Charlotte lurched to her feet, body humming with rage, hands fisted at her sides, the wolf back in her eyes. And this time it looked like she wasn't going to let it go. "No," she said. "Never."

"Look," I said, "it's not that I want to. You've done a great job." Wow, Syd. Way to make her feel cared about and all that. "You've been there for me when no one else was." Better. "But I care about you very much, and I don't want to see anything happen to you."

"If you send me away, I will die." Oh, the guilt and drama.

"I'll break the bond to save your life," I said. "Whether you like it or not."

"No," she said. Whispered. Breathed. "If you do so, I will die."

So not drama. "You mean, it will actually kill you?" What the hell kind of screwed up magic was this?

She bobbed her head, hugging herself as she shuffled her feet over the fresh carpet, replacing the one she'd totaled. "When we served the Russian royal family, it was our duty to do so for life. We were assigned our very own life to protect. Since you are a Princess, and a leader, I had to bond myself to you." She shrugged, like this wasn't some huge news she was dropping on me. "I'm tied to you for as long as you live. For as long as I do." Her human eyes pleaded with me to understand even as my heart sank. "It's not just about protecting you, now that we are connected. Your power feeds me, keeps me safe. Protects me as I protect you."

"You siphon power from me?" I was on my feet now. "Like a leech?"

I couldn't believe I just called Charlotte a bloodsucking parasite, but I wasn't exactly a happy camper at the moment.

She winced but nodded. "It's how the bond works. As a reward for keeping you safe," she said. "That's how the *кодекс честі* is able to function. In order for me to protect you, I have to link to your magic. And, as a reward, I receive the benefits of our association for as long as I keep you alive."

"Like what?" Okay, okay. I was wrapping my head around it. And it wasn't like she was taking power, not really. At least, I'd never felt weakened. In fact, I'd only grown stronger since she and I met.

"Longevity." She dropped her arms, shrugged. "Your immortality is mine, too."

Interesting. And one more person I'd have around. Though the thought of having my bodywere with me until the end of time kind of gave me the heebie jeebies when I thought about it for a second.

"This is a mess." I turned away from her, shaking my head. "I suppose there's no way around it?"

I glanced back to see her shivering. Miserable again, just lovely.

"I'm sorry," she said. "I should have told you."

"I guess you should have before you decided to create the bond in the first place." I went to her then, hugged her gently and, after a moment, she hugged me back. "We'll deal with it," I said. "And we'll find a way to free you."

Charlotte tried to protest. "I don't want to be free."

"Forget it," I said. "No way I'm staying tied at the hip to you for ever and ever." I winked. "We'd end up killing each other."

Charlotte's shy smile answered me. "It is my honor to serve."

"And your right to have a life." I pulled away. "We'll

talk about it when this is over."

She didn't answer, but she didn't have to. Probably thought I'd just forget about it.

Not this time, wolf girl.

"Just do what you can to keep your temper, okay?" I turned away from her, heading for the door. Charlotte caught me just before I reached it.

"Where are you going?" The wolf was back.

"Out," I said. "Without you."

She snarled and shuddered. "Among the vampires."

"I refuse to hide in here," I said, "while Mom argues and the Queens bitch and Margaret finally decides if it's worth it to cross the vampires." I shook out the heavy skirt of my dress, bits of wolf fur shaking free. "The little show we gave them earlier should hold them off. And at this point all I've done is freak out or look weak. I'm going to have a nice, long look around until it's time to show them who they're messing with."

Charlotte was right beside me when I jerked the door open. Sigh. Fine. "Temper," I snapped.

She bobbed a nod. Well, at least she'd be with me and I could keep an eye on her.

The two vampires guarding my door actually shrank back from me as I swept my way out and down the corridor. They followed, but kept their distance as I spent the next several hours climbing staircases and looking at paintings and tapestries, trying to keep myself occupied while scaring the pants off anyone who looked at me the wrong way.

Most of the vampires vanished the moment they spotted me, though a few did their best to flee with dignity.

"This is the Wilhelm seat," Charlotte said, pointing to a floor to ceiling portrait of a stunningly beautiful woman with the deepest shade of red hair I'd ever seen and piercing green eyes that seemed to leap from the canvas. "Yvette," she whispered, as though the dead vampire Queen could still hear her.

"I'm surprised Batsheva hasn't taken it down yet," I said.

Charlotte turned from it, face hard. "Perhaps she's pandering to the vampires in her clan. Yvette was a horrible soul, but her vampires adored her. Feared her. But were loyal to a fault."

All but Sunny. She'd broken out of the clan years ago, I seemed to recall. But why?

I turned to move into the next corridor only to see Celeste hovering at the corner, watching me. My vampire whispered in my head, telling me to bide my time, hold my temper, while the vision of a burning house, the fire magicked to devour despite our attempts to put it out, hovered in my mind. The screams of the dying inside. The final whispered words sent to me by Martin and Louisa Vega, killed because they knew too much.

By Celeste. Who stood before me, undead and unhappy.

"You owe me three lives," I said.

She jerked on a lock of her long hair, the old habit still with her. "Their losses were of no consequence," she said. "Sandra Crossman was dead weight in the coven and the Vegas... well, witches who poke their noses in where they aren't welcome are bound to meet a nasty end sooner or later."

The thought crossed my mind, cogs spinning, things falling into place even as I spoke the words aloud. "The Brotherhood," I said. "How long have you been working for them?"

She laughed at me then, tugging motion turned to stroking as though her hair was some beloved animal. "They accepted my help the day after your grandmother killed my leader."

The Purity battle? That long ago? Celeste would have only been a teenager.

"Is that how you met Batsheva?" I knew she left our coven when she and Mom were young.

"Through the Brotherhood," she said. "They've been watching you for a very long time, Sydlynn. You and your little family." A snicker. "Who do you think sent the Chosen of the Light to Wilding Springs?"

Demetrius. Speaking of nuts...

"Nice of them to saddle you with a narcissistic

psychopath." I smiled sweetly. "You must be having so much fun handling Batsheva these days."

Celeste flashed her fangs. "You've never been a fraction as clever as you believed, girl," she said. "There is so much going on, you have no idea."

"Such as?" Wouldn't be that easy. Not with Celeste.

She just smirked and went back to her petting. "You'll find out," she said. "When it's too late."

My magic hovered, so close. This. Freaking. Close. I was ready and, to my surprise, so was my vampire.

Damn, I hated interruptions.

Demetrius scuttled to Celeste's side, blue eyes flickering to me and back to her again.

"They are done," he said, singing his words. "Done, all done now." He pointed at me. "They want her."

Celeste paused, glared. I stood there and glared back. And just when I thought I'd get what I wanted, for her to make the first move, she laughed again, tossing her long hair aside before striding off, brown dress rustling.

Coward.

Chapter Eighteen

Though Celeste made a retreat, Demetrius still hung close, eyes watching her as she rounded the corner at the end of the hall before he did a happy dance, spinning in place.

"So, good news?" I started to follow Celeste, Charlotte behind me and he quickly kept pace.

"Very, very," he said. Danced again. Clapped his hands before covering his mouth with them, eyes huge. "Quietly," he whispered.

Right. He scampered off before I could comment I wasn't the loud one in our little conversation. I decided to take it slow, even though I wanted to run to the throne room and thank the Queens for their questionable hospitality before blowing this place.

Despite—or maybe because of—Demetrius's enthusiasm, my gut told me it wouldn't be so easy.

If I had real doubts, they were answered by the look on Mom's face the moment I entered the throne room and began my parade down the center carpet. From Sebastian's grim expression to Sunny's tight-lipped anger, Uncle Frank's crossed arms and even Margaret's frustration, everything screamed bad news for Syd. But the happy, even cheerful smile Batsheva fixed on me was the worst of all.

At least Pannera didn't look cheery either. I had that to keep me warm.

"All right," Margaret said in her bracing voice. "About time." She tapped one foot on the stone, hands on hips until I came to a stop in front of her. "We've come to a consensus."

"We have not," Mom said.

"We *have*." Margaret let her arms drop. "You, Sydlynn Hayle, have possession of vampire property. And while I agree with you said vampire property is, in fact, a personality, a life of its own," my vampire sniffed at "its", "and the right to choose, both clan leaders demand the return of this power." She held up both hands to silence me, though I didn't move or try to speak. "Since this power can't be forcibly removed from you, as that would break treaty law," Batsheva's smile slipped a little, "it has been decided you will remain here, in the custody of the vampire clans, until a time the personality or power or whatever you want to call it can be safely removed or chooses to leave you." She puffed to a halt, cheeks red while a bubbling mass of burning began in the very bottom of my feet and slowly rose to the back of my throat. "You will choose a clan to join so, through your connection to the vampires, the essence you carry will be part of all of them."

"I swear to you," Mom said, power crackling in her voice, "the High Council I command will not stand for this ruling."

Margaret spun on her. "What do you want me to do, Miriam?"

"I want you to do your damned job," Mom shot back. "Defend a witch in your territory."

"I've done so." Margaret's face pinched into petulance. "To the best of my ability."

"You've caved to the prattling of spoiled children," Mom said. "You do understand you're forcing me to take matters further."

Margaret paled, two pinpoints of red on her cheeks, looking like a flaky old woman who'd seen her day. "You wouldn't."

"I will." Mom straightened to her full height. "I will declare war over this."

As much as I loved my mother for throwing it all in over me, the look of triumph Celeste let slip at Mom's pronouncement told me everything I needed to know.

This was exactly what the Brotherhood was counting

on. So I had to stay.

But I couldn't stay. Trapped in a vampire clan when I wasn't really a vampire?

"If that's your decision." Margaret cooled to all new levels. "But I've fulfilled my obligations."

"Obligations." Mom snorted. Mom never snorted. "Run back to your soft life in London, Margaret, and bar your doors and your delusions from the truth. But if you are too weak and afraid of what might happen if you actually took action, I'll do it for you."

"My territory," Margaret said. "My final word."

"We'll see." Mom gestured to Pender, his grim face dark even as he stepped forward instantly. "Alert the others we're leaving to raise the Council."

He nodded once, backed away again, face distant as Mom continued.

"You had better hope none of your people find themselves in need of help in my territory," she said. "I promise you, it will not go well for them."

"Don't threaten me unless you're ready to act on it, Miriam." Margaret gestured herself, Elliot coming to her side, though I could tell by his posture and the sad look on his face he was less eager to do her bidding.

"Oh, I'm absolutely ready," Mom said as Pender came back to us and nodded to her. "And so is my Council."

Sydlynn. The vampire inside me whispered my name. *This cannot be.*

I know. I drew a breath, tried to look empty and bored. *I'm on it.*

"Thank you for your careful consideration of my case," I said. The two witches' heads snapped around, Mom and Margaret both staring at me like they'd forgotten where and why they were. Pannera's eyes showed some interest while Batsheva sat back with her usual smirk. Elliot's eyes met mine, his need for this to end well almost as bad as Margaret's.

Mom was right. They were weak, both of them. Complacent. How long had they ruled without having to act, to do anything aside from playing their parts? I almost felt sorry for them and hoped there were strong leaders who could take over for them when things went downhill.

And they would go downhill. Fast and hard.

I pushed on. "I accept your terms, but need a few moments to consider my options."

Mom's mouth dropped open even as Margaret grunted and looked away. I refused to meet my mother's eyes, instead staring Pannera down.

"Of course." Elliot stepped forward, motioned for two Enforcers, his, to come to my side. He turned to Batsheva then. "A room nearby where the coven leader might retreat?"

Nice choice of words, but I let it go. Batsheva waved with nonchalance while Piotr bowed, mocking me with his smile, his eyes. He'd recovered from our little teleportation trip. Looked like I let him off too easy.

Pity. I'd have to rectify that.

Chapter Nineteen

I imagined all the horrible things I could do to Piotr as I followed him, faithful Charlotte at my side, wishing for my demon and her very creative imagination. She always made plans for destruction so much more delightful.

And bloody.

The antechamber was plush, soft chairs and a deep sofa, a low table full of decanters and trays of food. Vampires ate, with gusto, if seeing Uncle Frank devour a burger was any indication, and wine was a favorite. But it wasn't likely this food was here for me. Probably for the two Queens.

Knowing that made me lose my appetite.

Mom didn't leave me alone for long, barging into the room, slamming the door closed on a very angry Margaret.

"You can't possibly be considering this," she said.

"Mom." I hugged her. "You have to let me go."

Her instant argument hung between us without her even saying a word, but I shook my head and released her.

"No, Mom," I said. "Don't you see? The Brotherhood isn't just after a war between vampire clans."

Mom shuddered a little. "I know," she whispered, covering her mouth with one hand, a hand that trembled, cold and white as any vampire. "I can't believe I let the argument with Margaret go that far."

I grasped her hand, pulled it down, held it, warmed it between my own. "I have a plan, okay? I promise. But you have to go. Before something happens we'll all regret and the Brotherhood will love."

"I can't just abandon you." Mom pulled away from me, bunching the sides of her cloak in her fingers. "I just can't, Syd."

"I won't be alone," I said. "I have Sebastian. Uncle Frank and Sunny." I turned and smiled at the weregirl beside me. "And I have Charlotte."

I count as well, I believe, my vampire sent.

You totally do.

Mom nodded and resisted all at the same time.

"You remember the trial?" I sank to one of the cushions, eyeing the food though there was no way my stomach would welcome any of it at the moment. "I wanted you to run, to defy the Council and witch law and get the hell out of there. You asked me to trust you. And I did, Mom. Even though I thought you were going to die. All I'm asking is for you to do the same."

She smiled at me, blinking moisture. "That was different," she said. "It was our law, witch law. You're facing something we have no experience with or control over." A single tear escaped her eye. "And you're my daughter."

I took her hand again, touched her vampire magic. Felt Gram and Sassafras latch onto me in a sudden rush of emotion. Mom had clearly been filling them in.

You get your ass back here. Gram's mind vibrated with fury. *Right. Now.*

I'm with Ethpeal. I could almost see Sassy's tail thrashing. *We'll deal with the fallout when it happens but, for now, just cut and run.*

Since when did a Hayle run from anything? I didn't mean to be cruel or harsh or for my words to cut, but I was just as frustrated as they were with one difference. I was the one who had to deal with the mess. *I'm not going anywhere and the three of you had better just suck it up.*

Mom quivered beside me. *What are you going to do?*

It doesn't matter. Better that she didn't know. *But you all have a job to do yourselves, so you'd better get cracking.*

Cleaning house. Gram grunted.

Damned right. I hugged her then Sassy with my mind, the vampire power doing its best to connect with them. *I don't want even a sniff of the Brotherhood anywhere near our coven by the time I get home.* I glared at Mom. *And that includes all covens.*

Mom nodded, brusque, tears gone, though her fingers clung to mine with a desperation I was beginning to feel. *Agreed.*

I don't know how this is going to play out. I hated to load them with more, but I had certain things that needed saying and I refused to do it when it was too late. *I love you all so much.* No crying. No. Crying. *I promise I won't do anything stupid.* Yeah, right. *But I have to see this through.*

Gram's goodbye was quick, abrupt even, as she cut me off. Sassafras was a little slower, but not much. When my aching heart tried to force me to sob like a child over their rejection, Mom hugged me.

"Neither of them knows how to say goodbye," she said. "For that matter, I don't either." Mom stiffened, threw her shoulders back, put on her Council Leader face. "Sydlynn Hayle," she said, "as your superior, I order you to come home safely."

Hard not to grin and salute. "Yes, ma'am."

She left in a swirl of lilacs, the scent clinging to my dress, my skin, the part of my mother always taking me back to childhood.

No. Freaking. Crying.

Good thing I had a distraction. The sound of grating stone made me turn around, a small hole appearing in the wall below a tapestry as Demetrius eased his way into the room with a big grin on his face.

"Perfect, just perfect, isn't it perfect?" He hopped up onto a chair and bounced a few times.

"Glad you see it that way." I sank down again, depression setting in. Demetrius stepped down and came to hover at my feet, still beaming.

"Joining her clan," he said. "So perfect. Couldn't have asked for nicer perfect, not at all."

"I'm sure Pannera will be delighted to have me." Sucked, but not like I had a wide variety of choice. At least she wasn't two cracks from shattered like her fellow Queen.

"Oh, nonononono." Demetrius clutched at the hem of my dress while Charlotte hummed a warning. "No, you musn't."

Um, what? "I'm joining Pannera's clan," I said.

"And when you attack Batsheva," he said, fear in his eyes, "your own clan will kill you for beginning a war."

I guess I hadn't thought this through all the way after all. Not like me.

Yeah, right.

Dread formed a roiling, painful ball in my belly while Demetrius leaned in close, whispering.

"You must do it," he said. "Only then will you be able

to challenge her. You have no choice. You must beg Batsheva to allow you into her clan."

It finally happened. I'd died and gone to hell.

Chapter Twenty

Demetrius didn't give me time to wallow in my sorrow.

"You will join her," he said, madness in his eyes, but cunning too. And the cunning I trusted. "You will be her responsibility."

Charlotte chuffed softly and I caught her actually laughing. Not a little laugh like she sometimes allowed to escape. She drew a breath and began to howl, slapping her knee with her open hand, wiping tears from her eyes as Demetrius grinned at her.

Clearly I was missing something.

"Brilliant," Charlotte choked. "Just brilliant."

"I'm all ears." I looked back and forth between them, patience so thin I could poke a finger through it.

"She will be forced to protect you," Charlotte said while Demetrius bobbed his head and wheezed a laugh.

"Meanwhile, you can gather power and plot to kill her and no one will say anything."

What kind of screwed up system was this? "So if I'm outside the family, she's off limits, but if I'm one of hers, I can kill her and no one will give a crap?"

Charlotte let out another deep, belly laugh. "As much as I hate to sound like the troll, he's right. It's perfect."

Demetrius ignored Charlotte's insulting nickname. "All are expecting you to choose Pannera," he said. "You have friends in her clan, at least. Family even, of your own. Batsheva believes you will make yourself an easy target for her by joining the one side you will be unable to act from."

"Vampire rules are so tricky," Charlotte said, humor fading, concern returning. "So many things to remember. Without acting openly, she could arrange it so you stepped over a line you didn't know you couldn't cross and BAM." She slammed one hand down on the back of the couch. "Pannera would be forced to kill you and share the essence."

"And you can believe Batsheva would ensure she took the lion's share." Demetrius's blue eyes spun in crazy circles, as though sounding coherent meant sacrificing more of his sanity. "This will blow her mind." He burst into giggles, bouncing on his haunches.

Sounded better than my plan, which, despite what I told Mom, wasn't much of one. And included what these two just told me not to do. So, Batsheva.

Well now. The possibilities were delicious for making her life miserable if she wasn't able to harm me.

Demetrius dug in his pocket, pulling out a flat metal box about the size of a deck of cards. He flipped it open, showed me the glittering powder inside. I instinctively pulled back, but he snapped it closed and pressed it into my hand before Charlotte could stop him.

"What remains of hers," he said. "Last resort. Not sure if it will work. But worth a try if you have to."

I clutched the thread of hope in my hand as a thought came to me. "My crystal." I leaned toward him. "I need my crystal." Not just a touch of hope now, but a surge of it so strong I almost felt my demon. Wishful thinking, but still. I had no proof it would help, despite my previous experience. I also had no proof it wouldn't.

He frowned a little, but bobbed his head. "Might work," he said. Brightened. "Might work."

Good enough for me. "Can you get it?"

He hesitated. "Difficult," he said.

Like I cared. "It's in the top drawer of my wardrobe at home," I said. Blushed.

Underwear drawer. Couldn't go there.

Demetrius finally smiled again, whatever he'd been thinking of worked out in his damaged brain. "I'll fetch it," he said.

Awesome. He scampered off, waving to me before

diving into the hole in the wall and pulling the small stone door shut behind him.

Castles and their secret passages. Reminded me of the vampire mansion back home. Which just made me homesick.

Sigh.

I stuffed the box into my corset, feeling the cold metal warm to skin temperature, shoving it down as far as I could so I wouldn't accidentally open it and breathe more of the stuff in.

This could work. If that was the case, why did my vampire sound doubtful? *Though you must be careful. Those laws he spoke of, the convoluted nature of vampire society, worries me deeply.*

How much do you know? Might be an advantage having her with me at this juncture. I knew the vampires wouldn't expect me to have much knowledge.

Not enough. She shifted around inside me, restless with frustration. Felt so weird I wanted to squirm too until she fell still again. *I had brief glimpses of vampire life with Sebastian and his clan, a few insights, but nothing that will help here.* Bummer. *Still, I do think this is our best option of the two.*

Grim and grimtastic. Yeah. Story of my life.

"What if they demand you actually become a real vampire?" Charlotte was on her feet, prowling the room.

Never going to happen.

You already are, the vampire said and I repeated it to

Charlotte who shrugged and continued her patrol. *I am you and you are me. You can't become any more a vampire just by dying.*

Nice to know. Considering I had no intention of finding out what dead was like on purpose.

Time to face the music. I rose, went to the door. Set my hand on the latch. *Are we ready?*

As we can be under the circumstances.

I reached out and hugged the vampire inside me for a moment. *Thank you.*

She seemed startled, took a second to respond. *For what? I've only caused you trouble since I emerged from the cave.*

No way, I sent. *I can't imagine life without you.*

Head high, a pleased vampire essence musing inside me and a very nervous weregirl at my back, I opened the door and faced the two Enforcers.

"I'm ready," I said.

The bowed, backed out of the way. Allowed me to lead our little procession to the black carpet, to march the length of the throne room and face down the two vampire Queens, one staring and cold, the other near giggles in anticipation.

"I have made my choice," I said, using my Mom volume. "I will honor this decision, on one condition."

Margaret sighed. "Get on with it."

It all hinged on this. If they demanded I become a vampire, I was running. Screw that.

Deep breath, Syd. "I remain as I am, and not be forced to become undead."

The vampires protested, of course they did. Not really a "oh, wow, really, you want me to die?" moment or anything.

I let them run on, eyes fixed on Margaret. And then, when they'd worked themselves into a froth, I let my vampire out.

She glowed, a star, a shining beacon, rippling through me as she spoke.

"She is already more vampire than any of you," she said with so much contempt I almost ruined it by breaking her hold and laughing. "This is not up for debate. If you choose to insist on her joining the ranks of the undead, I myself will begin this war. And I will finish it."

Margaret's eyes narrowed, but she nodded. "Agreed."

"Council Leader!" Pannera was on her feet. "This is not your choice to make."

I don't know if Margaret was just sick of the situation or if Mom had finally gotten through to her, but whatever the reason, she spun on her comfortable looking shoes and pinned the vampire Queen with her heavy stare.

"You've pushed me," she said. "And I've allowed your little game to unfold. But don't think I won't take steps, Pannera. This has gone as far as I'll allow it. The girl remains as she is."

Girl. Eye roll. At least she shut Pannera up. The vampire Queen hissed softly, but sat down again, hands steepled before her as she stared at me with hollow eyes.

Let her hate me. The feeling was growing to be rapidly mutual.

Batsheva on the other hand, just nodded and flipped her hand at me. "Agreed," she said.

"Now," Margaret turned to me. "Your choice?"

I could feel Sebastian trying to reach me, Uncle Frank. But Sunny was oddly quiet. Probably because, of the three of them, she trusted my judgment the most after all we'd been through.

Hoped I wasn't about to make her doubt my sanity.

"As much as I'm sure you'd make a fine leader, Pannera," a little heavy on the sarcasm, but who knew with vampires how much it took and I wanted to get my point across. "But I've decided to do things a little differently." I locked eyes with Batsheva who scowled, sitting up straighter while Celeste stared through slitted eyes.

Got them both, it seemed.

"Your Majesty," I said with a little curtsy, "I formally request you allow me to join the Blood Clan Moromond."

Oh, how it hurt to say those words. But the hateful look on her face was worth it.

Chapter Twenty One

Batsheva immediately demanded a recess of her own and, through another heaving sigh, Margaret granted it.

I wasn't alone in my chambers long before company rushed in to ask me if I'd been knocked from my rocker.

"You can't do this." Sebastian swept into the room, sweeping toward me, hands out. He gripped my shoulders, shook me ever so slightly, though the pressure of his hold told me just how agitated he was. He was nearing vampire strength, not be-nice-to-the-frail-witch-girl strength. And though I understood his concern, I had no desire to test the limits of my immortality under friendly fire.

I didn't get a chance to free myself. With a growl and a swipe of her arm, Charlotte knocked him back, away from me. Sebastian's eyes flared white a moment, fangs showing, his quick reaction to her protection also letting me know he wasn't happy.

Not even a little.

Charlotte just bared her teeth, sliding between us, the wolf coming out in her hands, the shift of her shoulders, and though I couldn't see her eyes, I knew it rose there, too.

This was no time for friends fighting friends. If there was ever a time for that.

"It's okay." I touched Charlotte's arm, felt her calm a little. "Back off, Sebastian. You of all people should know better than to come at me like that after the time she's had."

He did retreat, face settling to his normal handsomeness. "Forgive me," he said, voice deep and harsh. "I didn't mean to put more pressure on you, Charlotte. Considering what you've been through."

She nodded quickly, backed up until she stood behind my right shoulder.

Buddies again. Yippee.

Sunny seemed the only one who wasn't about to freak on me, so I focused on her, refusing to meet Uncle Frank's disapproval just yet as he hovered near. Not for the first time I understood no matter their relationship, how much they loved each other, she was his superior and, for vampires, that meant a lot, I was learning.

Wait a second. Did that mean when they got married they'd be equals?

How interesting.

"You have a plan." Sunny came to me, hugged me gently, even leaned forward to squeeze Charlotte's hand. I loved that about Sunny. So generous.

"Of course." I just wished it wasn't dependent on a very damaged Demetrius Strong. But I wasn't telling them that. Or how much my plan seemed to change moment to moment. Fly by the seat of my very airy pants, that was me. "I already talked to Mom. You're just going to have to trust me."

"We do," Sunny said. "But we worry."

"You're going to challenge her." Sebastian's hands tightened into fists. "You understand our laws well already."

"I had a crash course," I said. "And there's no way I'm staying put, not like this." I waved my arms around, indicating the castle, the vampires, everything. "I have to find a way to end this, and killing Batsheva is the only out I can see."

Even Uncle Frank nodded at that, though his blue eyes seemed sad.

"Can we do anything?" His turn to hug me. I wasn't about to turn him down.

"I'll let you know." I released him to find Sebastian staring at me. "I promise."

"What will you do with the power once you've won?" He shook his head, a little smile on his lips. "I've known you only a short time in my very long life, Sydlynn Hayle, and yet I cannot imagine any scenario in which you and your particular brand of luck and magic can fail." Nice of him to say so. Boosted my confidence a fraction. "So I ask again—what will you do with the magic of your new clan when you're through?"

"I haven't decided." I didn't mean to sigh, to sink to the chair next to me, to show them any kind of weakness, which might make them worry more. My only job at this point. No need for all of us to be in a lather. But I just couldn't help it, not with the giant task I still had ahead of me looming behind a beautiful face and insanity.

"You can't lead," Uncle Frank said. "You have a coven to take care of."

"I know," I said. "I'm working on it. Look," I climbed to my feet, squared my shoulders, put on a brave face I almost believed myself, "this will go one of two ways. Well, or down the crapper so fast you won't even know I was here. In either case, I want the three of you to stay out of it."

They all paused, thought about it. Nice to be loved, but seriously.

"I'll kill that bitch the first chance I get," I said, "while she's forced to keep her hands and arms inside the ride at all times. Easy peasy."

Sunny's frown told me, okay well, not so easy, but it was Sebastian who spoke. "You may not need to worry about Batsheva herself," he said. "You are correct she won't be able to harm you once you've been adopted into the clan. But that isn't true of other vampires in your family."

Well, that would have been nice to know. "Open season, huh?"

Uncle Frank crossed his arms over his chest. "No way, this is ridiculous. You're going home and the hell with the Queens."

Sebastian reached for my hand and held it a moment, ignoring Uncle Frank. "Missteps can happen easily," he said, "and the smallest slights can be seen as a reason for battle. But they must have a reason to fight you. Do you understand?"

"So they can come up with some stupid excuse, but if they just attack it's a no-no?" More rules. My head felt like it was going to explode.

Sunny laughed softly, without humor. "We are the masters of nuance," she said. "These rules we abide by keep little networks running, but can trip you up without understanding why. And we could easily tell you ours, if we had several years, but those of this clan are different. And change all the time." She shuddered and looked away. "This is why I hate court."

"Your personal clan isn't like this." I felt a little relief when Sebastian shook his head.

"There are moments," he said. "But I've never

allowed it in my own family. But even I must bear it here, under the hand of my Queen."

"Well, it's not like I haven't been down this road," I said. "Demonicon isn't a happy place either. Only they don't need a reason to challenge you."

"Except on Demonicon they only take a portion of your power," Sunny said, voice soft and grim. "Here, if you lose, they strip you of your magic and blood and leave you out in the sun to die."

So, a little more extreme, then.

"I need access to my power." I squeezed Sebastian's hand, getting to the point I'd almost forgotten I had to make. "Which means clearing away the control this powdered crystal has over me."

His forehead furrowed. "I remember," he said. "The night we found Cesard. It is the same substance?"

So quick. "You got it," I said. "Can you help again?"

Sebastian nodded without a spark of hesitation, his power entering my mind. I felt him this time, his doubt and concern, his anxiety he was betraying his Queen, but he didn't stop, the spirit magic animating his form reaching far inside me to link with my own.

The internal bite was harder this time, giving me an instant headache making me cry out, but the wave of spirit power flowing outward from it healed me almost immediately. Where once there was silence, I now heard a roaring in the distance, felt thrashing and clawing, the sound of uncontrollable weeping stilled and turned to shrill screaming of my name.

The hum of the family magic was strongest, reaching for me with so much longing I found tears on my cheeks when I pulled free of my internal review and smiled up at Sebastian.

I was still partially blocked. Whatever Demetrius did to me this time around, whether a stronger dose or a different one, the vampire's bite was only able to open me up about a quarter of the way. But I could feel them again, hear them, my demon finally settling though she continued to pick at the wall holding her back while Shaylee calmed and poured earth magic into the gap between us.

"Not complete," I said. "But thank you. This will do for now."

Until I had the crystal. I hoped. I could only keep my fingers crossed the crystal would have the same clearing effect on the powder as it had with the sorcerer's shields back at the Brotherhood house. As for cleaning my system out permanently, I'd have to figure something out after this particular minefield went kablooey.

I'd hold my awakened power in reserve until I needed it, but when I did, and when I had full access again?

Those Queens could just look the hell *out*.

Sunny and Uncle Frank left shortly after. Okay, Sunny left, dragging Uncle Frank who still looked like he was going to grab me and run off with me. Nice sentiment, and I might have let him if Sebastian's bite hadn't given me hope.

I smiled up at Sebastian as he released my hand, expecting him to go after them, only to feel him loom over me, fingers once more gripping my shoulders, though this time without fear.

Nope, totally different emotional trigger behind this particular contact. I didn't get a chance to gasp a breath as he bent over me, pulling me against his hard, broad chest, the lace at his throat tickling mine as he pressed his cool lips to my mouth while his magic wove through the vampire inside me.

He'd kissed me before. Once. On the lips. After I'd saved his life. That was something. Or I thought it was at the time.

Um, yeah. That was *nothing*. As his hands slid around my back, one pressing against the lowest ties of my corset, the other flat in the center between my shoulder blades, sparks of power danced between us at every point of contact. But not shocks, nothing so disruptive. These flickers of energy sped up my heart, made my breath come faster, air I breathed into lungs that didn't require any.

His tongue ran slowly over my lower lip before he pulled away, eyes burning with two points of white light before he let me go.

"Be careful, I beg you," he said, hoarse and rough, before spinning and leaving me there.

Panting. Hands pressed to my heaving bosom, I kid you *not*, just like some idiot girl in one of my trashy historical romances.

Yum.

Chapter Twenty Two

I know I should have been much more focused on what was happening around me as I was led out of my chambers by a pair of vampires, once Batsheva had enjoyed her little recess, and toward the throne room instead of thinking about Sebastian.

But oh, my, my, my. Those lips. That magic. My body still tingled.

So much for Quaid.

Who said that? I turned my head a little as we passed the entry to the main room only to catch sight of a black-robed figure behind a statue. One white hand swept the hood back a little, Ameline's crystal blue eyes locking on mine.

Choke.

We need to talk, she sent. *Watch your back.*

I couldn't think fast enough to latch onto her, nor, I

supposed, did I have the power. And then I was past her, every pair of eyes on me, including Mom's and Margaret's.

Did I dare mention Ameline was here? And what did she want?

Watch my back. Since when was the ice princess herself on my side?

So much churning going on, I needed a moment to reorder everything, but didn't get that moment. Though I wasn't the only one who needed time to think about my choice, from the look on Batsheva's face when I faced her again, she'd figured out a way to turn my decision to her advantage. Or at least thought she had, because she smiled and nodded to me in what I can only assume was gracious welcome as she gestured for me to come closer.

"Our clan will be richer for your presence," she said. "We wish you welcome, Sydlynn."

Batsheva will kill you the moment she can. Ameline's mental voice was as cold as the rest of her.

Duh, I sent. *Since when do you care?*

She laughed. *Don't start thinking we're besties*, Ameline sent, the vampire in her as icy as she was. *But you have something I want and I will not allow Batsheva to have it. Or the Brotherhood.*

What do you know of the Brotherhood? Leave it to Ameline to have more information than I did. Irked me to no end.

I said we'll talk. Her amusement was as plain as it was

chilly. *But believe me when I say I'm here to protect you and the vampire essence you carry. For now, you have an adoption ceremony to endure.*

She wasn't kidding. A short ceremony in what I could only guess was Austrian or some other language I didn't speak involving the vampires bowing to Batsheva over and over again and I was suddenly swept forward by Piotr's hand on my back while Charlotte growled and twitched next to me all the way to the foot of the throne.

Flawless. Not a crease or a blemish or a wrinkle to be seen on the vampire Queen's face. But no matter how beautiful death had made her, to me Batsheva would always be ugly.

Her power was nothing to sneeze at, I had to admit, as a wave of spirit magic rose from her and engulfed me. I had a moment of real fear, a flashback to the beach and almost drowning. I felt the same way, the pressure on my lungs to take a breath, the head-over-heels rush of primal strength, though it was only my insides enduring such treatment. The vampire essence grasped onto me and steadied me even as Batsheva's power gripped me tight in a band of pressure I'm sure was far more than necessary.

One thing was clear. The ancient spirit energy she commanded was flawed, tainted by centuries of influence from vampire Queens with only their own ambitions to please them.

Yes, the vampire sent. *Precisely. Before I attached to Cesard to preserve myself, I was pure. And thanks to you and your magic, I am again.* She shuddered. *Another reason why I will never join her, or the other. They are no longer me, Syd.*

There was nothing to say, not when Piotr gripped the back of my neck and shoved me forward, offering my throat to my soon-to-be Queen while Charlotte's growling turned to huffing whines. She had to hold it together. There was no other choice. And she did, bless her.

Somehow, she did. Even when Batsheva, lips split in a horrible smile, bent and pressed her lips to my skin. My pulse pounded, the cold of her mouth raising goosebumps along every inch of my exposed flesh as the tiniest of pinpricks broke the skin.

The worst of all of it, the most hideous part, was the sucking. I wanted to strike out at her, disgust and rage boiling, my demon clawing at my insides so hard I worried she might hurt us both.

I'd endured a lot of things in my lifetime. But having evil personified drink my blood with her cold, clammy lips locked on my bare skin took the cake, cutlery, plates, kitchen and house.

Which I'd burn down if it would remove the memory.

She pulled away at last, just when I was sure I couldn't do it anymore, lifting her arm toward me with a lazy smile, her tongue sliding out to lick her ruby lips, my blood staining her white, white teeth.

I'd never stop shuddering. Neverneverneverneverneve.

Her white wrist lifted, her own fangs cutting the skin at the pulse, a single drop of blackish blood oozing to the surface to pool between her tendons.

"Your blood mingles with ours now," she said. "Time for ours to live in you."

Hell no to the gazillionth power. No one mentioned drinking her damned blood from her ewie arm while everyone watched.

Oh. My. Swearword.

Piotr forced my head down and I let him. No way was I going to be able to do this on my own. Eyes squinched closed, bile already rising, I parted my lips over the pool of blood and drank.

I wish I could say it was gross. But the vampire part of me saved me from the disgustingness, showing me the light inside her blood. And yet, there it was, the taint, the filth under the brightness of spirit.

It was all I could do not to puke in Batsheva's lap.

Piotr released me the moment I did as I was required, backing away so, when I was done, I rose on my own power, glaring into the Queen's eyes.

"Be welcome," she said. "Beloved child of Moromond."

I couldn't wait to kill her ass.

Chapter Twenty Three

And that was that. Ceremony over, all said and done, nothing to see here, move along.

Margaret looked impatient, clearly wanting to zippity-do-da her way back to Delusionland. But no way was she going while Mom still hovered, her Enforcers gathered around her in a tight, angry knot.

Mom, I sent, feeling the rush of her relief when she felt my magicks were partially at my disposal. *Just go. It's cool. Go.*

With a firm nod and a flash of blue power, she did, her Enforcers with her, so fast Margaret grunted at the rapid departure before waving irritably at the lot of us.

"Behave," she snapped. "Or else." Then, she gathered up her own posse and left.

Wow. Effective. Wish I'd thought to try telling the Queens not to hurt me.

Snort.

Batsheva turned in her throne and glared at Pannera. "Your turn," she said, all illusions of niceness, as thin as they were, vanished with the witches.

Pannera simply reclined further in her own seat, a little smile on her stone face. Did wonders for her beauty, though I highly doubted she smiled for the right reasons anymore.

Their particular battle was going to have to wait. Charlotte still growled beside me, the low hum of her unhappiness putting my teeth on edge and I wasn't the only one. Batsheva turned her sharp-eyed attention from her fellow Queen and focused on my wereguard.

"As your ruler," she said, smirk returning, "you must obey me. You understand this?"

I was not going to like what she said next. Was *not*.

"I order you to eliminate the dog clinging to you." Batsheva sat back then, hands pressed together as she cackled in glee. "Personally."

I'd felt compulsion before, the urge to act, driven by some power or another's need for me to pay attention. But I'd never felt anything like this. As I drew a breath to tell her where to stuff herself, a deep, burning sensation began somewhere in my guts and spread outward, the pain growing as each second passed until I stood clutching my stomach and gasping for air, still fighting the need to turn and rip Charlotte's throat out.

Honestly? If I hadn't had my demon, Shaylee and the family magic holding me back, I would have killed the girl without hesitation and been left to cry over her dead body later.

Yet another reason to be grateful for my multiple occupation and to hate Batsheva from the bottom of my heart.

Instead, I spun, sucking in air, and gasped a name. "Uncle Frank."

He disappeared in a rush of shadow only to reappear at my side while Batsheva's—dear elements and all that was clean and beautiful, *my*—family of vampires hissed at him.

"Take her." Wow, I managed to squeeze out two more words while the world closed in around me, black-edged, my insides devouring themselves one burning bite at a time.

He didn't hesitate, nor give Charlotte a chance to argue. His fist lashed out, caught her in the jaw. The weregirl crumpled with shock and hurt on her face, into his arms and, as I fell to my knees, he shuddered into darkness and vanished.

Taking Charlotte with him.

The pain went the moment she did, blessed relief as I huddled in a puddle of skirt with both arms clutching myself, panting over the carpet while Batsheva laughed.

Two footsteps sounded next to me before hands

touched me gently, lifted me to my feet. Sunny's eyes flashed with fury as she spun on her old clan, sparks cascading from her hands as she gestured toward them.

"How far you've fallen, my old family." Wow. I'd never heard that level of disgust in someone's voice before. She must have been boosting the feeling with magic. And it looked like it was working as the vampires on Batsheva's side winced and flinched from my beautiful friend. "Yvette, our mother, she was hideous, but she led us clearly and with foresight." Sunny barely spared a glance for Batsheva, the Queen spluttering on her throne, but I kept a close eye both on her and Celeste who hovered behind the throne.

Sunny let me go, taking another step forward while I wavered, but held my feet, strength returning. "To allow this travesty of a leader in your midst, to accept such a sub-standard Queen to rule you." She shook her head, disappointment the chastising of children who had let her down. "Revolting."

What was funny? Most of the gathered vampires seemed to agree with her. Which led me to believe Yvette wasn't the only one who Batsheva influenced with the power of the Brotherhood.

Batsheva spun on Pannera. "It's time you take your foul-mouthed underlings and left my castle." Nice to know Sunny got to her.

Pannera didn't move, still smiling a little. "You invited

me here on good faith," she said. "We are both to share in the essence of our creation. When you approached me with this plan, it was a partnership. Are you now planning to betray me?"

Batsheva thudded back against her throne, glaring.

"If that were the case," Pannera said as she leaned slowly forward as though in answer to the other Queen's retreat, "I would have to declare war. And you don't want that." Pannera laughed. "Even Yvette was smart enough to know peace meant prosperity."

Vampire games. Like reindeer games, with fangs.

Seriously, were they this close to war all the time?

How sad, my vampire sent before quietly retreating inside me and going silent.

This was worse than Demonicon. At least there they were outward about their attack methods. I knew where I stood. Vampires? Diva drama Queens, literally, pushing each other back and forth, a pair of whiny cheerleader captains who just happened to have enough power to make it a problem for half a continent.

I was sick of their crap already and it had only just gotten real.

Celeste whispered in Batsheva's ear and, though the other woman waved her away with clear irritation, she finally smiled back at her rival.

"Here we are ignoring the guest of honor." She refocused on me.

Oh goody.

"Indeed." Pannera turned to me, too. They had to pick now to find a common enemy? I would have preferred to stand back and watch them tear each other apart.

I wondered if anyone would back me if I yelled, "Cat fight!"

"A feast." Batsheva swept to her feet while I shivered from the reference. As long as I wasn't on the menu. "A banquet the likes this castle hasn't seen in an age. For you, Sydlynn."

Right. For me. For the show, she meant.

At least I wasn't dead yet. Bonus.

She wasn't kidding, though. By the time we sat down, it was well after midnight, but my vampire clock didn't seem to care. And my empty stomach was happy to sample some of the multiple dishes delivered to my gold-edged plate. The company I kept didn't encourage my appetite, Piotr glowering on one side while Celeste sat like a stone statue on the other. But at least I had Sunny, Sebastian and Uncle Frank across from me so I had a nice view.

I didn't bother asking Uncle Frank how Charlotte was when he arrived back just before we sat down at the table, now spread in the center of the throne room, to dinner. It didn't matter. She was safe and, if I survived this, would punish me when I got home.

Piotr isn't all bad, Sunny's mind touched mine. *But he is misguided and very loyal.*

Misguided, huh? *Do you think he might be under influence?*

She nodded, hiding it by smiling at Uncle Frank as though he'd spoken. *I do.*

Which means they all are. Suspicions confirmed, or at least solidified.

Or were. She touched her hair, eyes drifting sideways, further down the table. *Yvette was horrible, Syd. Don't get me wrong. She played this game like no other Queen, had been at it even longer than Pannera. But she, too, was loyal to her family. Anyone, from the most powerful to the lowliest could count on her to stand for them in times of need. She was a brilliant leader, if a sick and twisted soul. But she was my Queen and I had her confidence for many years. For Batsheva to defeat her, she must have had access to powerful magic.*

Oh. Right. I filled her in quickly on what Demetrius told me and, for a moment, I worried Sunny might blow our secret little conversation.

She did what? Choked, furious.

I'm sorry, I sent. *I forgot I told Mom. Not you.*

It was a long time before Sunny reached for me again and when she did, her mind was cold. But not because she was angry with me, I knew it right away.

I'm going to kill her myself, she said.

You can't, I sent back. *You won't survive, remember? You're not of this clan anymore.*

She squirmed in her chair, eyes finally meeting mine. *I'm counting on you*, she sent. *No mercy.*

As if.

Sunny spent the rest of that long and tiring banquet filling me in on the vampires in the room. My family. They were a bunch, that was for sure. From murderers to thieves and bandits turned to vampires, Yvette seemed to have had a knack for attracting the worst common denominator to her clan and gentrifying them.

On the surface, Sunny sent. *Only on the surface.*

Which made me wonder about my friend's past. Not that I cared. She was on my side and I loved her. No matter what she did when she was a member of this sick collective.

Um, yeah. The same one I was part of now. Yet another lovely family to get to know. Though I had a quick laugh thinking what my Demonicon relatives would do if I arranged a whole-hog reunion.

Epic.

I tried not to give in to the growing doubt I felt, that I'd chosen the wrong side after all. There was nothing I could do about it, not now. I did catch Pannera staring at me, and knew if I wanted to switch sides she'd probably go for it. But I had a plan and I needed to stick to it.

I just needed Demetrius to come back with my crystal.

Batsheva ended the banquet abruptly, rising and

leaving as though bored with the whole thing. I could only guess her mind had a limit now that she was around the bend. It was Celeste who stood and clapped her hands, declaring the feast over.

I didn't exactly feel safe being escorted to my quarters by my "family", but no one gave me a choice. I guess I shouldn't have been surprised to find we took a few wrong turns along the route and ended up in a part of the castle I didn't think I'd seen before.

Dragging the new girl out to kill her, were they?

As my mind worked over a few ideas on how to deal with the problem, I happened to glance to my left through a doorway, surprised to find I was in the same section Charlotte and I explored earlier, the one with all the portraits. But the woman staring back at me from a giant canvas wasn't Yvette this time.

Nope. But now, from a distance and with shock filling my mind, I saw the family resemblance.

Holy.

No time to act on what I'd just learned or even think about the repercussions. Not when I was forced to halt in the middle of the corridor because the two vampires ahead of me had turned and were grinning at me with their fangs hanging out.

"Far enough," one of them said. Did I know him? Irrelevant. Been threatened and attacked by one crazy vamp, been threatened and attacked by them all.

"This is for Nicholas," another snarled behind me.

I laughed. Didn't mean to. "You'd better talk to Sebastian about that," I said. "Looks like you bunch were handed some inaccurate information." Batsheva and her lies. Tiresome.

That actually made them pause. "You killed him," the first vampire said.

"No," I spoke slowly, keeping it casual though my heartbeat sped up in preparation for the inevitable. "Sunny did. Because Sebastian couldn't bring himself to put down his own mad brother."

"It's true." Sebastian melted from the darkness, Sunny on one side, Anastasia on the other. "Sydlynn had nothing to do with Nicholas's death."

I was still expecting a fight. But nothing happened. My vampire guides looked first angry, then sad, turning as a group, vanishing into shadow.

I wanted to say something, an apology for calling Nicholas crazy, even though he was. But Sebastian didn't give me a chance. Instead, he held out one hand to me.

"Come," he said. "Our Queen would like a word with you."

Chapter Twenty Four

"You need to be wary." Sebastian's voice was soft, low, but came through clear enough. "As much as I have trusted my Queen in the past, I'm not as certain of her intentions anymore."

Sad. I reached out and linked my arm through his, the two blonde vampires swaying in their ball gowns ahead of us. "I'm sorry," I said, really meaning it.

Family. Who else could hurt him so much?

His hand settled over mine, pressing my fingers into his arm. "This entire situation could get out of control very quickly," he went on. "Neither of our clans is meant to be in such close proximity for such an extended period."

A bomb waiting to go off, in other words. Well, at least if they were fighting each other, they might forget about me.

"Batsheva is up to her old tricks," I said. "Not like she'd shift tactics now anyway, since her mind's gone bye-bye. She's lying to her vampires."

Sebastian shrugged. "There's nothing we can do to stop her," he said. "She is Queen."

Well, wasn't *she* special?

We didn't have far to go, the door to Pannera's quarters flanked by half a dozen undead, Uncle Frank among them, though he looked pretty unhappy about it. I reached out and squeezed his hand on the way by as Sebastian guided me through the hastily opened door and presented me to his Queen.

"Your Majesty." He swept into a deep bow, leaving me behind as he went to her, bending on one knee to kiss the back of her offered hand. She reclined on a well-stuffed divan, leaning forward to greet him as he pressed his mouth to her skin.

Naughty thoughts. Naughty. And envy. Oh yeah.

"Sebastian." She freed her hand from his grasp and ran her fingers through his black hair. "We've missed you." Her accent made her seem so exotic. And she was stunning. No wonder he looked at her with adoration.

Hey. Jealousy? Yeah, you. Take a flying leap off a high cliff already.

Besides, she owned his ass. For all I knew, she was influencing him through their bond.

Sure, Syd. That was it. Um-hum.

It didn't take Pannera long to shift her attention to me and, for a moment, I was actually furious at her for her lack of caring and horribly disappointed for Sebastian as she pushed him aside and gestured for me to move forward. She didn't care about him, about anyone.

Time to get my bitch on.

I didn't move, held my ground, though Pannera's small smile of welcome faded. Tough patooties. She could chew on my particular brand of stubborn and see how she liked the taste.

"Very well then." Pannera sat back, eyes shuttered, face cold all over again. "I can see you won't react to kindness. Let me instead warn you what a great mistake you've made." She paused. "And that I'm ready to correct that mistake."

Sure she was. "For a price," I said. "I'm not paying it. Anything else?"

Was that frustration? Wicked.

"We both share the same desire." Pannera sat as still as a statue, rather creepy with just her lips moving. "To destroy Batsheva. I understand why you joined her clan, your reasoning. But if you had trusted me, I could have helped you dethrone the usurper." One perfect eyebrow arched. "Now, thanks to your choice, you've left yourself defenseless in a family who will destroy you for what you carry."

Like she wouldn't if it meant getting what she wanted.

"Thanks for your concern," I said. Didn't roll my eyes. Mostly.

Pannera surged to her feet, her anger showing at last, vampire appearing for a brief nightmare moment before she settled, poised and flawless again. "Yvette and I may not have had lost love between us," she said, "but I despise the vile Batsheva and will never consider her an equal." Pannera licked her lips slowly. Way to creep me out. "You are a fool for trying to kill her alone. You will never defeat Batsheva, not with all of the power of your clan behind her."

Okay, this time I did roll my eyes as I felt my own fear fading into disdain. "You have no idea how old that is," I said. "You think I haven't heard the big scary crap before? Do you have one sweet clue what I've been through, what asses I've kicked in the last three years?" Not to sound pompous, but she was sounding more pathetic by the moment with her empty threats.

Pannera hissed while Sebastian kept his eyes locked on the floor, though his wide shoulders twitched. "She owns you now, fool," she said.

"For the moment," I said. "But I'm not just the vampire who lives inside me." Why did everyone just assume I was alone in this? "I'll be ready for her. But will she be ready to take on a coven leader, demon royalty, a Sidhe Princess *and* a vampire born of the maji?"

Pannera's anger vanished, brows pulling together.

"Your power was supposed to be blocked."

"Yeah, best laid plans. Worked really well, didn't it?" Time to show off a little. I opened up as wide as I could, knowing I'd better make it good with what little I had. Shaylee did her best, driving as much earth magic as she had access to into the floor under my feet, the whole room vibrating a moment before my demon shot forward, squeezing through the gap, my vision tinted amber for a few seconds before she fell back, panting.

The ropes of family magic answering my call did the best, coiling around my feet and legs, rising to twine around my outstretched arm as I held it up like a pet snake before letting it go.

Pannera watched the whole show with her mask of stone firmly in place, but, when I was done, she nodded. "Everyone out."

Interesting. They obeyed her instantly, her fawning vampires fleeing as though she'd cracked them with a whip. Pannera reached out as Sebastian moved to leave and held him back. "Stay," she said. But the rest, Sunny and Anastasia included, vanished behind the closing door until it was only the three of us.

The vampire Queen sank to the divan, frown returned. "You will repeat this to no one." She glared at me, but this was a step in the trust direction. She had no way of compelling me. So I nodded and took the olive branch, just hoping there wasn't a scorpion hiding in the leaves. "I have been... concerned," translate: afraid, "in the past few months. Vampires have gone missing, no warning, no return of their power. But they are dead. Their bodies have been found."

"Return of their power?" What did that mean?

"When a vampire expires, their magic comes home to their Queen," she said.

Like coven magic. Okay then.

"So you think Batsheva is behind it?" Possible. Wouldn't put it past her.

"Thinning our ranks," Pannera hissed. "Preparing to attack."

Kay, she took paranoia to a whole new level.

"You have proof?" Not likely.

"Of course not," she snapped. "If I did, I would have attacked her long ago."

More Brotherhood meddling? So it made sense it was Batsheva. Or Celeste. This whole war thing was wearing on the vibrating thread of my one remaining nerve.

"It is her usual practice," I said. Filled her in on the last two times Batsheva and I butted heads. It was the cheater notes version, but she got the point.

"Then you understand how important it is she not come into possession of the vampire creation magic." Pannera suddenly warmed, coming toward me, her eyes drawing me in as though she somehow thought she could coerce me like one of her vampires. Or a mere mortal.

I had more than enough protections with all the power inside me I was able to brush away the compulsion and scowl.

"You bet," I said. "Just as important as keeping her," I pointed to my chest, "away from you, too."

Pannera snarled and spun, dress rustling as she paced away from me. "How can I get through to you, foolish child!"

Um, first off, drop the "foolish child" stuff. "What do you want, Pannera? That I'm willing to give?"

"Work for me." She stopped moving again, focus as sharp as the predator she was. "Keep me informed on your Queen's activities."

"And what do I get out of this little arrangement?" I could tell Sebastian wasn't happy, not even a little, but he held his place, head still down, frowning.

"I'll allow you to destroy her," the Queen said.

"Yeah, sorry," I said. "Already in the plan. Anything else to offer?"

A chair disintegrated under her furious hands into a pile of very tiny kindling before she settled again, hair undisturbed, dress perfect. "Hear me, Sydlynn Hayle," she said, beginning her little melodramatic show all over again. "If you take Batsheva's life and the source of her clan's power, I will do everything I can to destroy you."

Is that what she was worried about?

"I don't want that power," I said. "Or the clan. Okay?

Seriously, what is wrong with you people? How many times do I have to tell you I have bigger and better things to do than huddle in a drafty castle in the back ass of Europe and play dress up?"

Pannera snapped, coming for me, but I was ready and so was my demon.

Just enough fire. Vampires hate fire. I think I singed her.

Most awesome.

"I will kill you," she snarled.

"You want my life?" I shook my head. "Better be sure. It sucks most of the time. No pun intended."

Pannera managed to pull herself back under control. "You think I don't pay attention," she said, pacing back and forth in front of me like a caged lion wishing she could eat me. "You think I'm blind to the goings on in the world. I am not so foolish." She jabbed one index finger at me, really in a froth now. "I know well what it is you are becoming, and how close you are to completing your evolution."

"Then you have to know I have no desire to rule a clan." I glanced at Sebastian who finally looked up, face blank. No help there, but I knew his hands were tied. "I have the Brotherhood to deal with. You want my job?" I paused as she calmed, shook her head. "Unless you're working for them too," I said. "In that case, rules or no rules, I'll kill you right now and be done with it."

I thought she was mad before. "Blasphemy!" She didn't seem shocked at the mention of the Brotherhood, so someone must have told her about Batsheva. Sunny? Or maybe the overly observant Queen already knew. Pannera's vampirishness lingered for a long time. Hollywood had nothing on the real thing. I'd have bad dreams for weeks filled with images of the stunning Queen mingled with the hideous monster. "Never!"

"Good to know. If I can trust you." I met Sebastian's eyes. Was concerned he looked suddenly troubled.

"I will never work for the Brotherhood." Pannera's disgust was so real I had to believe her. "Yet another reason to kill Batsheva before she taints too many with her evil."

Agreed there.

"You've made yourself clear," I said, hoping this standoff would hold. "I won't take the throne and you won't interfere. I can handle Batsheva myself."

"You find a way to kill her and not become Queen," Pannera said, "and I will allow you to walk away with our creation magic." "For now" hung in her words, but she didn't say it out loud so I took it as a victory.

Mind you, the whole "let" thing was just going to have to go.

"Done," I said.

Chapter Twenty Five

Pannera sent me on my way with Sebastian at my side once more. Only now, when he walked beside me I wondered why he was with me—for me, or because she ordered him to watch me and report back to her?

I hated thinking about him like that. Sebastian was my friend and, if the kiss he offered me was genuine, maybe had the potential to be more. I couldn't bear to live with the idea that everything he did was suspect.

"I have my people placed carefully," he said as we walked, breaking my sad silence. "They will alert me if anything happens, but I can't do much more than that, especially after the sun rises." He slowed his pace a little, bending over me. "I'm sorry, Sydlynn. I should never have allowed you to risk your life to save me when I was host to the essence."

"Water under the bridge," I said. "I just hope you

know I'm not angry or anything. About you following orders." The memory of the pain my battle caused was enough to make me wince. "I'm just a little hurt knowing I can't really trust you now."

He stopped me, at my door, turned me to face him while two of Batsheva's vampires watched and waited. "You can always trust me," he said, voice thick with emotion, eyes full of intensity I couldn't identify. Or wouldn't.

This time when he kissed me his arms engulfed me, sweeping me up from my feet as his mouth warmed against mine. Though he had no heartbeat, I shared mine with him as my arms wound around his neck without my permission, the pulse of his blood keeping time with the thrum of each pounding beat.

And then he was gone, the two vampires long vanished, a pair of lunky mortal men coming toward me. One glance at the window showed me the rising sun and I knew, if our timing hadn't been off, it was possible things might have gone much further than I planned.

No way could I make room for another potential boyfriend. Not now anyway.

I went inside, sat down on the first chair I came across and forced myself to breathe. Kissing Quaid was all heat and passion, burning with my demon panting for more. Liam, on the other hand, was gentle but powerful, the deep and endless hum of the earth running through him.

Sebastian was another thing entirely. The sparking spirit magic was a game changer, as though his undead body took on the properties of my living one, creating very close to a perfect match to the vibration of my soul. Yes, I was aware the core of vampirism probably had something to do with it, but she wasn't talking and, as the sun rose and bathed my face in the first rays of morning, I didn't care.

Wow, that man could kiss.

"Was he really so delicious?"

Damn it, damn it! How did I let her get the drop on me like that? Stupid, idiotic—

I lurched to my feet, eyes sweeping the room, finding Ameline reclining in a corner, black cloak set aside, looking odd in blue jeans and a black leather jacket surrounded by the old world. I was so used to formal attire by now, seeing her in casuals added to my disorientation.

"What do you want?" I had my power back, yes. But was it enough to take on Ameline? She'd almost killed me more than once and I wasn't about to trust her as far as I could pitch her out the nearest window.

"You know what I want." Ameline's cold smile reminded me of Pannera. "But I needed to wait until daylight, so we could talk uninterrupted." She stood slowly, stretched, tall, slim body more beefed up than the last time I'd run into her. I saw well-defined biceps as she slid her jacket off, tank top revealing her cut and muscular shoulders. "How have you been, Syd?"

Small talk? She was up to something. "You can't have the essence any more than those vampire Queens," I said. "So get the hell out before I find out what your insides look like scattered on the floor."

She laughed, posed, like some kind of action hero from the big screen, all dark and dangerous. "We both know your power is diminished," she said. "Poor Syd."

Demetrius lunged from the bedroom, snarling and spitting at her, before darting around the furniture and coming to crouch at my feet. She frowned at last, though the expression vanished after a brief moment.

"I see you've traded one dog for another," she said.

"Don't trust her, don't, not ever." He clung to my leg, blue eyes huge and full of anxiety, body quivering with it.

"Not to worry," I said. "Never going to happen."

Ameline shrugged artfully, hands on her hips. "I have no illusions of friendship," she said. "Nor do you, I imagine. But I, too, oppose the Brotherhood. And that should count for something."

Not much. "You're trying to become maji," I said.

"I won't deny it." Ameline brushed back her long, black hair from her shoulder. "Whoever wins the race to evolution will rule everything. You must know that by now."

I didn't. And didn't want it. But she did, so I had to oppose her. Of course.

She took a slow step forward, running fingertips over the wood on the back of a sofa, pausing to grip it in her hands as she leaned toward me. "I need that essence," she said. "But I'm not greedy. I'll be happy with half."

"In exchange for what?" I might not have been very good at the follow through in negotiations, usually declaring refusal outright, but I was learning a few things.

"I help you kill Batsheva." She smiled, straightened, holding her hands out. "Mess cleaned up and we go on our way, leaving us both free to pursue our destinies."

She feels like the undead already. The vampire stilled as my mind agreed. When Ameline connected with me to warn me earlier, I'd felt the vampire in her then. *Ask her where the power came from.*

I already knew. She'd been working with Yvette's vampires before now.

No, the vampire sent. *It's more than that. Ask her.*

"What have you been doing with your days, Ameline?" I watched as she continued to drift around the room, keeping her distance, while Demetrius muttered and shook at my feet. "Hunting, maybe?"

"Maybe." She poured herself a glass of wine from the decanter I'd ignored since I arrived and swirled it before breathing deeply. "The vampire magic I've had access too hasn't been enough."

She's the one killing Pannera's people. The vampire sighed. *I can't go with her, Sydlynn.*

I loved it when we agreed on things.

"I've been siphoning a few of the weaker members from both sides." Ameline took a seat and sipped her drink. "Keeping them at each other's throats." Her laugh was as rich as the deep red wine in her glass. "It's been ever so much fun."

Ameline never failed to remind me of what a pleasant person she was.

"All of that is irrelevant now," she said. "I've been trying for some time to figure out a way to take the essence from you. Now I have an excellent opportunity for us both to benefit." Another sip, a slow wink. "I want to help you kill Batsheva before she gives the clan to the Brotherhood."

"I told you, I'm planning on destroying her," I said. "No help required. Thanks anyway."

Ameline looked like she was going to go on, but shrugged, stood up, set down her glass. "I know very well how stubborn you are," she said. "And when I'm talking to a wall." She returned to her original chair, slid on her jacket and robe without another word. When she was done, she turned to me with that same smile on her face, though her blue eyes were as cold as ever.

"But, I want you to remember," she said, "when the time comes, you turned me down."

Shrug. "Whatever."

"I'll be around," she said, pulling the cloak tightly around her. "If you change your mind."

"Ameline." I took a step forward, a sudden thought making me wonder. "If you want it so badly, why don't you just come here and try to take it?"

Those blue eyes snapped fire a moment before they narrowed just a little. "You're stronger than I am," she said. "Even with your power diminished, your vampire core could take me out easily. Besides," she flared with purple magic, "I want you to admit you are wrong. And I want you to give it up willingly."

Her laughter lingered long after she was gone, while I fumed.

Never going to happen. Even while my mind whispered I should never say never.

Chapter Twenty Six

If I was so adamant and sure of my plan—yeah, right—why did the idea of a little outside assistance from Ameline keep cropping up in my over-stressed brain?

Demetrius was pretty set on his opinions about her. "No, can't, worse than Batsheva, worse than Belaisle." He shuddered when he spoke the sorcerer's name. I didn't blame him, really. Liander Belaisle was about as smarmy and arrogant as they came, with serious dominance issues, if our brief encounter in his custody was an experience to judge from. "Ameline, she is hate."

And while I occasionally danced with the devil, I took his warning to heart.

Okay then. No Ameline.

"Is there a way to remove the powder from my system?" I sat so I'd be more on eye level with the man, still hunkered down near the floor.

"Yes, yes, yes," he said. "But you won't be happy. No, no, no."

Lovely. "Spill it."

He flinched, a whine escaping before he bobbed his head, silver curls swaying. "All of your blood has to leave you."

Well, the vampires would be happy. "And my crystal?"

He hugged himself, a little snarl on his face. "I'm going." Demetrius dodged away, running back for the bedroom and his secret passage before I even thought to ask him how he planned to get to Wilding Springs in time. He was a sorcerer. Nutty as a jar of peanut butter, but still a sorcerer. And I knew he wouldn't promise if he couldn't deliver.

Another hot shower did me good, though this time I was alone and felt the pressure of keeping myself safe without Charlotte to watch my back. I piled as much furniture in front of my door as I could before using a precious little of my earth magic to lock the wood in place between the stone casements. A quick search of my bedroom revealed the passage entrance, which I also sealed. Demetrius wasn't welcome to come and go when I was in the nude.

All I could hope was he'd fulfill his promise and bring me the crystal. If he was capable. If he had the means to get to my house and inside and retrieve the thing.

If, if, if. Maybe I should have been reaching for Gram instead.

I secreted the small box of powder into the back corner of the wardrobe, not wanting to have it with me but hoping my choice to hide it instead of carrying it wouldn't come back to haunt me. Worn thin, I then sat down on the edge of the bed, body heavy, a yawn escaping. So tired. Now that I had a moment to just stop and think, I could barely keep my eyes open. Promising myself only a few minutes to close my eyes, feeling as safe as I could considering the circumstances, I propped myself up into a sitting position on a pile of thick pillows and had a quick nap.

Sebastian's lips traced down my throat, over the soft skin of my shoulder and across the line of my bodice, pausing just at the edge of my heaving breasts.

"Beautiful one," he whispered, one hand sliding up my ribcage, points of spirit magic lighting me on fire with every spark, "you don't know how wonderful I can make your body feel."

He wasn't alone, Quaid, his bare chest dark from the sun, pentagram tattoo flashing with magic, crawled up the satin sheets toward me, dark eyes half-lidded, the heat of his power sliding under me, cushioning me as I vibrated from the pressure. "I love you," he whispered, coming to hover over my mouth, the delicious scent of him making me quiver. "Let me show you how much."

Liam slid in next to me on my other side, green glints of Sidhe fire dancing in his hazel eyes as the power of the earth rumbled through him and into me. "Our Queen," *he said, pressing his lips to my cheek as Sebastian sighed over me.* "My love."

"My Queen." *His tongue traced a path down my flesh before he stopped to meet my eyes with his adoring gaze.* "My love."

I rose from the bed, Quaid rising to his knees, catching my hand in his. "My Queen," *he cried.* "My love!"

Sycophants, pulling at my power with their need. Well, I didn't need them. I called up my vampire essence and destroyed them all with a single flash of lighting. Who was I to require anyone, anything, but what I had? What I was becoming? All powerful, not a Queen, far more than that as I shed my mortal form and blazed across the Universe as pure light, an iridescent glow of absolute power—

I tumbled from the pile of pillows with a gasp, thrashing a moment before I realized I'd been dreaming. Groaning, rubbing my face with both hands, I fell backward into the mess I'd made of the bed and tried to pull myself together.

One glance at the window shot me out of bed in a flash as I rushed for the closet and something to wear while I tore at my hair in a panic. Dusk. Damn it, I'd slept the whole day away.

I thought you needed to. My vampire sounded contrite at least. *And you were having such pleasant dreams.*

I bit back a swearword or two and stopped my frantic

search for a dress I could put on without help. *You watched over me.* Not a question.

I always do, she sent. *We all do.* Rumbling from my demon and Shaylee, a soft hug from the family magic. *You're never left unprotected.*

Well, that was a bit of a take-aback. *I didn't know.* But wait, hadn't she said something about it earlier? I just hadn't paid attention at the time.

You do now. She paused. *Though I think we left you too long. Time to get ready.*

Now she told me.

I just managed to corral my hair into something that didn't look like I'd slept on it wet and shimmied myself into a corset and dress with a bit of magical help when someone knocked on my door.

At least they'd found some manners. Piotr stood on the other side, dressed as impeccably as ever, making me very self-conscious and wishing selfishly I'd kept Charlotte with me anyway. "Her Majesty is hosting another dinner," he said. "Your attendance is required."

If all they did was eat and drink and try to corner me now and then, this whole killing Batsheva thing was going to take forever. I was already primed and ready for a fight when, following closely behind Piotr so I'd have some warning, I felt the air displacement preceding the arrival of vampires.

They were so damned blatant about it, I couldn't keep

my temper in check. *Sebastian*. No panic, just focused irritation as the four vampires circled me, Piotr fading into the background with a salute before he disappeared.

Sydlynn. You're in danger.

Why did he sound more worried than I felt?

Probably because the moment the vampires attacked me, mine came out to play.

And she wasn't holding anything back.

Chapter Twenty Seven

I didn't kill any of them. Pretty sure. But not one of my four attackers were able to get up when my vampire was done with them.

The little skirmish only increased my annoyance, ramping up as I stalked away from their groaning complaints and stomped my way to the throne room. It had been converted into a banquet hall the night before and, from the look of the well-laden tables, this was to be another prolonged evening of dining and dissembling.

Not if I had anything to say about it.

Piotr hovered near Batsheva, standing behind her chair, glaring at me as I stormed my way into the hall and up to the Queen who was responsible for my safety.

"This piece of garbage," I jabbed a finger at him, "and his little friends attacked me on my way here." Piotr didn't react, though Batsheva's smile pulled into a false frown while Pannera watched with interest. Sebastian half-rose from his chair, but his Queen waved him back.

Careful, he sent.

I was done with careful. "What are you going to do about it?"

Batsheva tapped her fingertips on the tabletop. "You seem to have survived the encounter," she said.

"They didn't give a reason for their attack." One of the damned rules of theirs. They'd used them against me enough since I got here. Now it was my turn to throw it in her face.

Piotr's eyes narrowed before he looked away. Forgot he was supposed to accuse me of something, did he? Or maybe he didn't think I'd been paying attention.

Arrogant ass.

"Of course, such an outrage must be addressed." Batsheva turned to Piotr. "Did you attack Sydlynn?"

"I did not," he said.

Okay, technically he didn't. Damned sophistry. I ground my teeth together and fought my demon's temper, coming through quite nicely even if her power wasn't. "You come near me again," I snarled, "and I'll make sure you suffer for a very long time."

I'm sure it wasn't in Batsheva's plan, if she really had one, to let Piotr slip his leash, but that was what happened when a crazy woman tried to control a clan of the emotionally unstable undead. Piotr lunged for me, teeth bared, my vampire lashing out, the pulse of her magic knocking him back to fall into Batsheva's lap.

Silence. The entire room fell deathly quiet. Until Pannera laughed.

Loud and cheery, a belly laugh of joyful proportions. And her clan laughed with her.

Not all of them. Sebastian looked like he wanted to yell at me while Sunny just sat, tense and alert, Uncle Frank unhappy beside her.

I didn't mean to humiliate my Queen in public. But she had it coming.

I have no idea who threw the first utensil, only that it ended up embedded in one of the lesser vampire's cheeks. On Pannera's side. Clearly, the Moromond clan didn't take kindly to being laughed at. More quiet, even Pannera, though I felt the rumble rising beneath the silence, barely having enough time to whisper "oh noes" to myself before the place went ballistic.

Pannera was already on her feet, her power sizzling through the air in an attempt to minimize the damage, but her vampires were in too deep of a frenzy. Sebastian had been right, one match was all this powder keg needed to explode.

And I'd struck the spark.

I ducked out of the way as two vampires, now in full undead mode, clawed and bit at one another, flashing in and out as they clung and fought. Two more rolled past me, thrashing on the floor, inhuman howling piercing my eardrums until I had to press my hands over them to save myself from a rupture. Sebastian flickered out of shadow at my side, one hand on my arm, but I pulled free as Batsheva shoved Piotr out of her lap and stood slowly, a huge grin on her face.

Pannera was alone, it looked like, the sole Queen trying to put out the fire. And as much as I felt a little guilty for causing the mess, part of me hoped they'd destroy each other so I could just go home.

One last crash of magic sent all of the fighters to their knees, including Sebastian and my uncle, though somehow Sunny retained her feet, Piotr's throat squeezed tight in one hand.

Pannera's magic retreated back into her as the stunned gathering began to slowly, sullenly, retreat to their seats, masks of civility gone, but forced to behave. For the moment. When she fixed me with her vicious fury, I almost let my vampire out to show her what real power was.

"You see what you've caused?" Pannera gestured around her. "The strife and conflict? Our clans have lived in peace," snort, yeah right, "for centuries until you stole the source of our magic."

Oh, she did *not* just go there. "You want the essence, Pannera?" I held my arms wide. "Come and get it. But until you stop accusing me of something that's none of your damned business and never was, you can either give it a go or shut the hell up."

Batsheva's loud, slow clapping prevented Pannera's answer. "My vampire is correct." Stress on the "my". Gross. "It's clear you've orchestrated this entire event by refusing to leave my castle. You wish for our clans to fight, is that it, Pannera? To take the essence for yourself?"

This was getting way out of hand. Rumblings from both sides started up again and I knew, barring a miracle, if the vampires started fighting again, they wouldn't stop until there was a winner.

And I had no illusions whoever won would then turn on me, facade no longer necessary.

I had to act.

"Batsheva." I turned to face her, drawing the power of the essence out, letting everyone see it again, reminding them what I carried as clearly as possible.

Syd. Sunny's voice reached me, panic in her mind. *What are you doing?*

You know what I'm doing. I shut her off as I did my best to look all regal and stuff.

Syd! Sunny reached me through the block. *Wait, not yet!*

No more waiting. Not while Batsheva stared at me with her icy eyes and her smirk of a smile, Celeste scowling beside her.

Showtime.

"I challenge you for leadership of the Moromond Clan," I said.

Oh, Syd, Sunny said, now afraid. Very afraid.

Of what? I could win. I just needed the nasty ex-witch to hurry up and accept.

"No," Batsheva said. "I don't think so."

Chapter Twenty Eight

One would think my friends would have prepared me better. Told me everything I needed to know about this challenge business. Who knew Batsheva could say no?

You don't have any support in the family, Sunny broke through, voice low and anxious. *She doesn't have to fight you.*

Thanks so much for telling me before I made an idiot of myself, I shot back at her while Batsheva slowly stood. *Now what?*

Sunny didn't answer. But Batsheva did.

"Traitor," she said, joy in her voice as she slowly circled me, her vampires closing in while Pannera and her family fell back. All of them. Sebastian, Sunny. Uncle Frank.

Uh-oh.

"Strike one," Celeste said.

Syd, Sunny reached for me in desperation. *I'm sorry, this is my fault. I never expected you to challenge her so soon. Syd...*

you have to run.

I did not like the sound of that. Especially when the clan clustered closer, glowing eyes burning with white fire, fangs out, hissing and growling warning me I'd stepped in it this time up to my neck.

As long as I kept my head above water.

"Spy." Batsheva whispered the next accusation, turning to point at Pannera. "You think I didn't find out about your little pact with her?"

"Strike two." Celeste's smile was worst of all. I never saw her smile.

"Assault." Batsheva leaned close and breathed the word in my face, the coppery scent of her making me gag. "You attacked your own Queen."

What, that little lap dance with Piotr? That was an accident. Mostly.

Celeste held up three fingers, teeth flashing in the light. "I'm hoping you're tasty," she said.

Laughed.

"Bring the chains." Batsheva pulled away. "This vampire has broken clan law and will be drained of her blood before I strip her power." One icy finger ran over my cheek. "Personally."

Sydlynn, you have to run. Sebastian sounded as desperate as Sunny. *There is no other way.*

"Proof!" Sunny stepped out of the crowd, eyes flickering to Pannera who nodded, just a little. "I demand to see proof."

Batsheva spun and hissed at her. "You aren't of this clan," she said.

"Nor am I," Pannera said. "But I, too, want proof, considering the implications if you are permitted to take her power."

Celeste muttered something to Batsheva who waved her off, scariness gone, replaced by irritation.

"Oh, very well. Bring the informant forward."

A slim and lovely vampire, fear on her face but shoulders back in defiance, stepped up. I'd seen her before, one of Pannera's inner circle, wasn't she? She'd been there when the Queen and I had our little meeting. But Pannera banished everyone from the room… secret passage eavesdropping session anyone? After all, she wouldn't have technically been in the room. Vampires were so sneaky. "I shared this abomination's plans with the Queen," she said.

Pannera's eyes narrowed, power crackling from her hands. "My own blood," she said. "You dare defy your Queen?"

"I wish to join the Moromond Clan," the vampire said. "Where I belong." She met Piotr's eyes and smiled.

Soft. Innocent even. Full of love.

The bastard.

He gestured for her to come to him, taking her hand, resting the other on her shoulder. "My Queen," he said to

Batsheva. "I have promised Ellia the reward of our family blood if she shares everything."

Batsheva nodded, all gracious and sickening like. "Proceed, my dear."

I was going to barf any second now.

The young vampire woman proceeded to explain how she'd listened in on the rest of my conversation with Pannera. "They are working together against you, great Queen," Ellia said.

Pannera said nothing, face blank. Seriously? I was a little tired of the whole statue act.

But her message was pretty obvious and I had to believe it was true I was on my own, no matter what I agreed to when Pannera asked me to spy for her.

No help for Syd. Typical.

"You have assaulted your Queen with power," Batsheva said, turning to me. The crowd of her vampires rumbled in answer. "Spied on her for another clan." A deeper response, full of hate. Why did they hate me again? Someone to focus their own self-loathing on, maybe. For letting this psycho kill their beloved leader. "And the worst of all offenses, you have challenged your Queen for her place as leader of your clan, though your clan rejects you." A roar from a hundred throats.

So. Not. Good.

"I will now strip you of everything you are." She hovered close to me, her power reaching for me even as the vampire inside me drew tight and closed to protect herself.

"Not before I claim the same right." Batsheva spun with a snarl as Pannera spoke. "Either adopt that thing," she jabbed a finger at the girl who'd betrayed her, "or hand her over to me."

Batsheva showed her true colors in that moment. As did Piotr.

"You can have her," she said, airy and uncaring as Piotr shoved Ellia toward her clan. "I don't want another traitor in my midst."

The girl staggered, spun to stare at the vampire she thought loved her. We all saw it, his slow and painful rejection of her as he allowed his smirk to return. I watched Ellia crumble, accept what she'd done before turning to her Queen.

"Forgive me," she choked. "I was misled."

No mercy in the vampire world. Before she finished speaking, Ellia was surrounded. I held my breath, wanting to turn away, heart in my throat for her. Yes, she'd betrayed Pannera. But she didn't deserve to die for it.

It's our law, Sebastian sent. I was saved the view of the girl's take down only because I stared into his eyes. But her screams, the shrieking cries of pain and cracking of bone, tearing of fabric as they pounced on her and sucked her dry, would stay with me for the rest of my life.

When it was over, I forced myself to look. The

shrunken mummy lying on the rough stone beside the banquet table looked nothing like the girl she'd just been. Now Ellia was merely a bag of shattered bones, not a drop of blood in her entire form, though her eyes remained, alive and terrified, as she was lifted by three vampires.

"Take her," Pannera waved them off, no longer interested from the bored expression on her face. "Put her somewhere the sun will find her in the morning."

"I hope you were watching," Celeste whispered in my ear, the brush of her hair on my back making me shiver. "You're next."

Chapter Twenty Nine

I ran. I had no choice, no recourse. I could have fought, of course I could have. But even if I won, Pannera would have attacked me next for the power of the essence, law or no law. Especially after our little conversation about me taking the throne should I win.

Even my vampire essence wasn't strong enough to take on two Queens.

But I knew better than to teleport. Instead, just as Celeste's hissing whisper faded from her lips, I reached deep, drew my demon as far to the surface as I could and tore open the veil.

I felt Celeste's hand on my neck as I tumbled forward into the narrow gap, barely big enough for me to squeeze through. Her grip slid, released as the veil slammed shut behind her.

I hoped she lost a finger.

Only problem was, my demon was now out of power and able to muster only enough to reopen the veil and toss me out before she lost consciousness. I staggered into the darkness, surrounded by trees, stumbling over a pile of rocks and to the edge of a very, very high cliff.

Panic drove me back from the edge to clutch at the trunk of an evergreen, panting and crying from fear.

—I'm falling and falling, the mountain passing to my left, the city of Ostrogotho growing larger on my right, heading for the Parade at terminal velocity while I fight to breathe—

It took me too long to recover, far too long, especially when I looked up and saw the castle on the next ridge, so close they would be on me in moments.

If they could track me.

I had no doubt they could.

"Ready to accept my help yet?"

I spun, found Ameline standing at the lip of the brink, looking down over the edge without fear. I hated her so much in that instant I lashed out with my vampire power. Would have pushed her over the edge if she hadn't stepped back and to the side in time my attack missed.

"I take that as a no." Ameline shrugged, jacket creaking under her black cloak. "Don't say I didn't offer." She paused as I felt the subtle compression of air displacement. A vampire. Two, more and more, all around me. Not on me yet, but they would be soon.

"You're sure?" She smiled and I lost it.

"You'd better run," I snarled. "Because when I clean up these miserable excuses for vampires I'm going to come after you."

Ameline laughed before touching her fingers to her forehead and bowing a little. "I'll be waiting."

She shuddered into shadow and vanished just as the pale, ghostly figures of Batsheva's vampires drifted into view, floating faces, shoulders, and claw-like hands glistening white in the darkness, closing in on me.

I begged my demon to wake, felt Shaylee prodding her with her own level of desperation, called up my family magic to feed her. But it was no use. She'd given me everything she'd had.

It wasn't nearly enough. But not her fault, not Shaylee's or the power of my witchcraft. Not my vampire's either. I'd failed them all because I just didn't think I could lose.

There was still teleportation. I let the vampire out. Time to blow.

"Stop." Batsheva's voice echoed from the trees as she drifted forward, Celeste on one side, Piotr on the other.

And everything stopped.

Oh, I tried. The vampire in me tried. But we were frozen, locked in place, no amount of help from Shaylee or my magic able to free me from that command.

Familiar faces appeared from the black, coming to stand beside me.

"Right to death," Batsheva snarled. "You're no longer welcome, Pannera."

The vampire Queen turned and met my eyes. "I told you this wouldn't work." She shook her head. "You little fool. You've doomed us all."

Thanks for the kick in the hee-haw when I was down.

"I will not abandon our only hope against the Brotherhood." Sunny stepped in front of me. "Or my friend."

"I won't leave my niece to be killed for your revenge and because you want to steal her power." Uncle Frank joined her, one arm around her shoulders.

"And I." Sebastian came to my side, reaching for my hand. "I owe her my soul."

Maybe if he'd let well enough be, things would have turned out differently. Because Pannera didn't seem to oppose Sunny and Uncle Frank's support of me. But the moment Sebastian touched me, jealousy crossed the Queen's face and sealed my doom.

"This is vampire law." She slashed the air with one hand. "My clan is ordered to leave. Immediately." She turned from my uncle, my friends. "All of you."

Sebastian's hand tightened on mine, his face contorting in pain. I pulled against his grip, freeing my hand before shoving him back. "Just go," I whispered, unable to speak louder for fear I'd beg him to say. "Please."

Pannera would kill them, I had no doubt. And since it was clear I was going to die in the next few minutes, no way was I taking three people I cared about with me.

Uncle Frank staggered from the weight of the order, reaching for me, but I stepped back, focusing on Sebastian. "Just take him and go!"

Sebastian, longing and agony on his face, grasped Uncle Frank's arm and shuddered into shadow.

They were gone.

Sunny turned to me, her own pain clear, but somehow resisting the order the best.

"I love you," she whispered. "And I will die with you. I can't leave you alone."

I hugged her, desperately. "I can't bear to think you died because of me. Please, Sunny, if you really do love me, follow your orders."

Okay, just to be clear here, I wanted her to stay. Hell, yeah. Would have caved in about half a second if she'd lingered any longer. She made it hard enough as it was to be brave when I just wanted to howl for my mommy and make her fix this.

My job. There had to be something I could do.

"You will leave," Pannera snapped, right in Sunny's ear. "Now."

My friend flickered, face twisting in pain. Fought it. And vanished.

Pannera spun on Batsheva. "This was your plan all

along," she spit her fury at the other Queen. "You had no intention of sharing the power. You manipulated me into challenging the witches and put my clan at risk." She slashed at Batsheva's feet with her power. "Don't think I will ever forget this. Or think for a moment we are done."

"I order you to leave my territory," Batsheva said with a sweet smile, "and never set foot it in again or there will be war between us."

Pannera stepped back from the pulse of magic joining Batsheva's words, sparing me one last flat, empty look before she, too, teleported away with the rest of her clan.

Leaving me alone.

In the dark forest.

With death.

Batsheva's smile didn't waver.

"Drain her," she said.

Chapter Thirty

Shaylee's keening echoed in my head as I was pulled to the ground and pinned under countless bodies. I fought them, screaming in answer to my Sidhe's cries, my vampire pushing them away over and over as the clan rushed in and struck me countless blows.

"Stop fighting." Batsheva's laughter followed her order as my body went limp and unmoving though my mind still tried to move my limbs. Even my vampire was still, Shaylee's crying now, soft sobs, her power reaching out to support me though she knew the same thing I did.

We were going to die and there wasn't anything we could do to stop it.

"Strip her clothing." Claws tore at my dress in response, slashing great rents in the fabric, pulling it free, exposed to the night air where I lay, shivering but motionless, looking up at the clear crystal stars while my brain spun in circles of panic.

But my heart... my heart was quiet. Still. Calm. And, as Batsheva bent over me, her long hair falling to brush my bare shoulder, I felt my mind retreat to huddle like a silent, terrified child and await our fate.

Immortal, yes. Invincible?

Well, I was about to find out.

"Feed."

They leaped on me, their fangs puncturing my skin, countless pinpricks of pain, some tearing the flesh as their cold lips locked on me and drew the blood from my body. Tears welled in my eyes, blurring the sky above, trickling slowly down the sides of my face and into my hair as I felt my life leaving me, the world drawing out, further, elongating as my heartbeat slowed.

Slowed.

Slowed.

I blinked once, sight dim, only vaguely aware now, though I heard her voice.

"Enough."

The pain was gone. I floated, almost happy. My vampire reached for me as Shaylee sighed softly and fell asleep, my family magic coiling around me before it, too, faded.

I'm sorry. I grasped the essence with the strength I had left, feeling her wind around me.

As am I. Believe I won't go willingly. And that I love you,

Sydlynn Hayle.

Love you too.

Batsheva's face blocked my view, darkness closing in around the edges. Even crying was an effort now. She laughed, the sound bouncing around in my head, reverberating as I faded farther away.

I felt her fangs though my body was cold. But only because she drew my vampire away, drinking what remained of my blood and, through it, the essence.

So. Hard. Clinging... feeling her slip away from me. Feeling me slip... away from me.

My heart beat.

Slowing.

Slowing...

A flutter of magic, a rush of power short lived as the last of the powder burned away, leaving me free.

Remember, Ameline whispered in my mind, *you owe me for this.*

A jolt of magic where once I was drained, enough to wake my demon, screaming, just the right amount she needed to tear at the veil. Batsheva shrieked at me to stop, but there was little of her blood left in me. No hold. I was free.

The veil was cold and soft and welcoming as I fell inside and into the darkness forever.

Chapter Thirty One

flash
flicker
spark
silence
black
quiet
nothing
Nothing.

Something?
I'm floating. Weightless. There is pain, but only peripheral, as though it's someone else's and I'm holding onto it for them.
But no. This is what it feels like to die.
I think I should be sad about it, but it's hard to feel anything. The world is a dull, soft place without edges and as I float, the pain fades too, leaving me alone.

Alone. As I always knew I'd be in the end.

That wakes something in me. I might be crying, but it hardly matters. No feeling sorry for myself in death. Won't do me any good.

You cannot die, Sydlynn Hayle.

I know her, the voice. The wavering image I can almost see clearly.

Iepa. *Her name is an effort.*

You are of the Undying, dear one. And you must survive.

She should have mentioned that to the vampires. Before they drained me.

Why are you haunting me? *She needs to leave. There will be a light or something soon, I hope. To show me where to go.*

You are still in the veil, *she says*. And you are very much alive. *Pause*. Well, alive.

I find myself snorting laughter, though I don't have the strength to make any sound.

Use the center of your power, the magic that has been with you your entire life. *She prods me, lets me feel what I'd forgotten.*

The blood of the maji. Pure creation energy.

Rise, my child, *she says*. Rise and heal and end this strife. You have much more work to do before you rest.

It's there, pulsing deep within. Patient, waiting for me to reach out and touch it—

My demon wakes, trills a call of weariness and agony. Shaylee breathes a sigh. My family magic stirs, trembles.

My vampire... is gone. But not completely. Residue remains, enough I weep for her and her loss. Enough to remind me, to make me hope. Even if it's just a little.

Very good, *Iepa says.* Now. Before it is too late.

Maji power winds through demon and witch and Sidhe and the barest breath of vampire, while in my pores, the hum of another power stirs. Cold. Colder than the vampire essence, hungry and yearning for something to devour.

My soul? Maybe. But for now, I use it for my purpose and hope it is enough.

The veil tears, a whisper of a gap, enough I can feel the real world on the other side.

Help. *So tiny that cry. So pathetic.* Help. *Is that the best you can do, Hayle?* Help, please. *No one is listening. No one will help you. Just give up.*

Just quit already.

Syd? *I know that voice, too, feel her reach for me while I sob in relief and the veil parts and I am falling, falling into Trill's arms while Iepa whispers in my mind.*

Be well, my child.

Chapter Thirty Two

Light wakes me. Trill's glasses catch a little of it, reflecting over her brown eyes as she says my name, but I don't hear her speak until long after her lips have stopped moving. Makes me giggle, her soundtrack is off.

Giggling hurts.

An old woman joins her, hair tight in a red kerchief though sprigs of steel gray peek out along the edges. She has a very large mole on the end of her chin and I can't stop staring at it.

More giggling. More pain.

Trill's lips move. Time passes. I hear her words: "Is she going to be okay, Nona?" Fear in her voice. Yes, in her face too, as she pulls away her glasses, her brown eyes clear to me.

Another face, this one with vibrant blue eyes, makes me smile. I open my mouth to say "Owen."

And pass out.

My body rocks back and forth, something soft under me, daylight streaming in a window over my head. Handmade quilt, the smell of the outdoors and cooking. The rumble of an engine, wheels over pavement.

Darkness.

"—brought her as fast as we could." Nona's voice, Trill hovering. It's night now, a light bulb overhead casting strange shadows. But the familiar feeling of magic, family magic, pulls me close and whispers to me as hands touch my face, lips soft on my cheek, faded blue eyes full of tears meet mine.

"Oh, girl," Gram whispers.

Fade to shadow.

Whispering, lots of whispering, hands holding mine, magic threading through me as my demon stirs, Shaylee sighing, my body on fire, burning, the pain rising until I cry out from it.

Then it's gone and I'm out again.

Flicker
Gram hovers, holding my hand to her cheek
Flash
Mom glows with power, Meira too, flooding my body

and lighting the room, casting their faces in an eerie glow

Snap

Liam's familiar scent, an arm around my shoulders, my head on his chest while a big, black face with glowing red eyes watches me from the foot of the bed

Spark

The rustle of fabric as Quaid rises from my side, black cloak with blue edges, strong hand releasing mine

Wake

Wake

Wake.

I opened my eyes. Found a pair of amber ones staring, a small, pink nose almost touching mine. Soft, silver ears perked, a single tail-thump striking my ribs.

"Syd," Sassafras whispered. "About time."

I lifted my arms, weighing ten times normal, and hugged him to me, sobbing into his fur while he murmured in my ear, amber magic pulling me close as he purred and purred away my fear.

"It's over," he said at last. "You're going to be okay."

I snuffled, letting him go, wiping my nose and eyes with the sheet, body coming alive and awake, no longer feeling like I had the house sitting on me.

Just my silver Persian. And he was always welcome.

My demon purred back at him, stretching and waking as Shaylee hugged me, my family magic bubbling. But my vampire, she who I'd lost, was gone, only a trace of her remaining.

I should have been happy to be alive. Home, in my own bed, and, if the feeling of the house beneath me was to be believed, surrounded and protected by the people I loved. The whole coven was here. Not in body, but in power, the thrum of their awareness all around me.

Why did I want to hide from them? Instinct pulled my power tight, lidded it and, despite my worry the other parts of me would protest, they didn't. They missed her as much as I did. Felt the guilt I felt.

Sassafras's eyes flared with power, but he didn't comment. Knew better. "I'll tell the others you're awake," he said, turning and leaping from the bed, running out the door to summon my family, to flood my life with people and their joy while my heart wept for my loss.

I crept out of bed and slunk down the stairs, slipping out the back door to perch on the bench alone, shivering in my pajamas, the sky over head full of pinpoint stars.

I suddenly hated the dark.

The screen door sang, padding steps approached. I didn't look up, didn't have to. Fluffy socks settled next to my bare feet, the sigh of her breath and the pressure of her on the bench disturbing my solitude. One wrinkled hand reached out and cupped mine as she sat back, our shared magic full of love, but holding its breath.

We sat there in silence for a long moment. Until I couldn't stand it any longer.

"How long?" My voice was still rough, my throat sore. More a croak than a voice.

"Three days." Gram's foot bobbed over her crossed knee. Pink and green this time. I loved her socks and never told her. Needed to. "Trill and Owen brought you back, them and their Nona." They found their grandmother and she was all right, no matter what the sorcerer Belaisle tried to make Trill believe. That made me feel a little better. And the memories I had of our journey, the rocking motion. Trill said they had an RV.

"They saved you." She sounded guilty. And I knew why. She would be feeling she should have saved me.

"Iepa." I said. "The maji." And one other, though I wouldn't speak her name. Would never acknowledge her help. I hadn't asked for it. Didn't want it.

Refused to believe Ameline had saved my life.

"How, Gram?" I met her eyes at last, tightness in my chest making it hard to draw air. "I should be dead."

Gram's eyes glistened in the light over the door, but her voice was steady when she spoke. "You should," she said.

"The vampire essence..." It hurt to think of her. "She said I was immortal, but not invincible. Was she wrong?"

Gram didn't say anything. I was glad. I needed to work this through on my own.

"She called me the Undying." My fingers flexed on Gram's. "Iepa. Trill did too." A massive shudder took me, the need to sob, broken and lost and alone. I felt the family now, crowded at the back door, wanting to come to me, holding back.

Giving me my space.

"Then it must be." Gram sighed, pulled on her grip, caught me against her, cheek on my hair.

Both of my hands rose, clutched at my chest without my consent, the empty hole inside me begging for what I'd lost. And though the maji power swelled and tried to fill it, there just wasn't enough.

Would never be enough now that I knew what it was like to be almost whole.

Gram had to have known where my mind was going. "You're safe," she said. "Home with us. Alive. And you have your marbles, yet." Unlike her experience. I wondered then if she resented my ability to survive, even when I'd lost my demon. But no, not Gram.

Not ever.

"You could leave things here." She sounded like she didn't believe what she was saying either. "Let Batsheva keep what she's stolen. Neither blood clan has said anything, though they both know you live."

Sebastian? Or spies. Whatever.

"I can't." Breathing was easier again when I spoke those two words, the tightness loosening, my body feeling lighter already.

"Is that the best choice?" Gram paused. "For your

coven?"

No hesitation on my part. "Yes," I said. "I've been here before. I needed my demon when she was taken from me," she hummed happily in answer, "and I need my vampire now." The jab of pain wasn't quite so bad. "If only because my coven needs me to fight the Brotherhood." I pulled free of her and faced her, found her nodding, sad but stern.

"All right then," she said. "Let's get you cleaned up and pay Batsheva a visit."

My heart sang in anticipation. Time to get my vampire back.

Chapter Thirty Three

I didn't have to tell them where I was going, what I was doing. The crowd at the door already knew. Backed off and let me enter, hands touching me, Mom hugging me swiftly, Meira, Liam. Uncle Frank almost crushed me he held me so tight, but I didn't mind.

"We should have stayed, fought harder." His words were muffled in my hair.

"You had no choice." I kissed his cheek and smiled. I could smile now that I'd decided what to do. "But I do."

Sunny next, trembling, teary, but full of love. "I'll never forgive myself," she whispered.

"Silly," I said. "I feel the same way about me. For putting all of you in that position. I should have just cut and run instead of trying to play their game."

Sebastian. He engulfed me in his arms, though his body was rigid. "I failed you."

Damn them, all of them, with their guilt. Though I understood it, of course I did. But I needed them to suck it up if I was going to go back and do what I had to.

"Enough," I said, with enough force behind it they all stilled. "We've been through a lot together." I looked up, saw Trill watching from behind Sebastian, her and Owen and their Nona holding back, giving the family room. "We don't always get to have happy endings." Trill's arm went around her brother as she leaned into her grandmother. "But we always do our best to finish what we start." She nodded to me, smiled as I turned to face the others. "Guilt and accusations and stupid mistakes be damned. I'm going to Austria to clean up a mess. Who's with me?"

"You're clearly off your rocker," Sassafras said, tail thrashing. "But Batsheva must be stopped."

Nods all around. Mom looked positively nasty. "I'll alert my colleague we're on our way," she said with way too much satisfaction in her voice.

Margaret Applegate was going to love seeing us coming.

I left them talking, planning, headed for the stairs and the shower I so desperately craved. Liam's hand caught my arm as he followed me up, drawing out a hiss of pain from my lips.

Not whole yet by a long shot.

He winced, let me go, eyes sad. "Please," he said.

"Think this through."

"I already have." He of all people, trying to talk me out of it?

"Syd." Liam rose another step, face level with mine, lips hovering close to my mouth as he ever-so-gently touched my cheek with his fingertips. "I won't survive if I lose you."

"Liam." Galleytrot's deep voice broke the moment between us. "Come."

I met the big dog's eyes, caught his slow nod. Knew he understood.

The water was lovely and hot, though the lights too bright. Not that I was photosensitive anymore, but because of how I looked. Sunken skin, pale and slightly green, dark circles under my eyes. I slowly turned in the mirror and forced myself to examine my skin, to look at each and every puncture, mostly healed but still visible, the faint scars left from my healing where the flesh was torn by vampire teeth, and the deep, round welts on my neck.

From her. Batsheva. Where she'd stolen my soul.

The need to kill someone, my hate, had never been so powerful.

My demon growled, but she felt hurt, anguished. Shaylee too, though she was as determined as I to return and take back what we'd lost. Even the family magic coiled inside me, retreating from my hate.

Deep breath. Let it out. Another. I hugged myself as I stood there, calling up my demon as she flashed amber in my eyes, Shaylee who wove around me with Sidhe power and the witch magic I'd rejected for so long flaring to life as it rose to shield us all.

Not alone, not by a long shot. And I refused to let hate consume me. To become what Demetrius knew of Ameline, what I did as well. Not when I had myself and myself and, yes, myself to lean on. I wouldn't become the woman I hunted or the one I had to face for the return of my vampire.

Their relief was as real as our need when the hard ball of rage released and let go. No need for it. Though I wasn't making any promises when I had Batsheva in my hands.

My robe, normally soft and lovely on my skin felt almost abrasive as I belted it tight and opened the door to cross the hall.

And thought of Charlotte. Panic drove a spike through me, my power whipping outward to search for her.

Found her in Mom's room, unconscious on the bed. Worn out or magicked that way, I didn't know. But she was alive and safe.

I'd done that much right.

We'd just see if she'd ever forgive me for it.

I knew my room wasn't empty before I entered, but I

was okay with my visitor. Trill sat on the end of my bed, hands folded in front of her, shoulders hunched a little as though expecting to be asked to leave. I crossed right to her and sat beside her, hugging her hard while her arms rose and hugged me back.

"Thank you," I whispered.

"You're welcome," she said.

We smiled at each other a moment before Trill sighed. "We can't stay," she said. "But I wanted to see you before we left. Alone."

I took her hand, feeling tears rise. "You saved my life," I said.

"Just returning the favor," she said. "But Syd, I didn't save you. Neither did Nona or Owen. When you dropped out of the veil, I was sure you were already dead." She shuddered softly as the image flared between us. I gasped at the sight of me, mummified as the young vampire Ellia had been when her clan was finished with her.

"There's no way you should be alive," Trill said. "Unless you're very, very close."

"The Undying." I nodded. "Iepa came to me in the veil. She told me I had too much left to do. She sent me to you, I guess."

"I've never seen anything like it," Trill said. "I'm just glad you're all right."

So I guessed I was invincible. At least, until I'd fulfilled the task Iepa had for me. Somehow, knowing it didn't make me feel any better.

"I will answer your call whenever you need me," she said with so much emotion I wondered where the girl I'd first met went, the angry, suspicious girl who, now I was willing to admit it, reminded me a lot of who I'd been not so long ago.

"And I yours," I said, hugging her again.

"Please be careful," she said. "I know you must retrieve the vampire essence, but remember. She's been tied to Batsheva's power. The taint may have affected her."

I hadn't thought of that. "We'll just have to make sure nothing of the Queen remains then," I said.

Trill smiled at my tone. "I almost wish I could be there to see you kick her ass."

Laughter felt good, seemed to heal me further. "I'll tell you all about it when I see you again."

Trill paused at the door, turning with a smile. "I meant to thank you," she said. "For our escort."

"Sorry?" Escort?

"Quaid." Her glasses flashed in the light, brown eyes full of mischief. "Though I was annoyed at the time, he made himself useful. Thank you for asking him to watch over us."

I grinned. "He can be an arrogant jerkasaurus," I said, "but he's helpful when he wants to be."

Trill laughed. "Once I put him in his place," she said.

Crap. I would have loved to have seen that.

She waved as she left. I closed the door behind her, turning slowly, eyes falling on my wardrobe, a sinking feeling in my stomach telling me something wasn't right.

The top drawer was ajar.

A quick search told me, though a little late to be helpful, Demetrius had succeeded in retrieving my crystal. Damn it.

Talk about terrible timing. Still, I could only believe he was back with Batsheva. So I'd track him down and take it back before I did horrible things to her.

Oh, so horrible.

My demon chuckled. Now that the blackness of my hate had gone, she and the rest of my carry-ons were more than happy to consider the possibilities.

I drew on as much of the family magic as I could while I dressed, trying to fill up reserves drained by the vampires. By the time I was done, the massive magic had fleshed me out further, the bags gone, my skin a more normal pink, though I was still thin, so thin.

Alison would have been really jealous.

Why did I think of her in that moment? My throat burned with the need to cry as I tightened the leather belt I needed to hold up my jeans, but there was no time to break down, not now. Later. Later, if I really felt I needed it. But I had a feeling when this was done, I wouldn't be the one in tears.

Mom's door creaked softly as I entered and went to the bed. Charlotte's body twitched as I settled on the quilt beside her. I could have left her behind, and probably should have. But she was as much a part of me as my vampire and I wanted her with me, selfish or not.

One touch and she woke, sitting up, hands grasping my arms, eyes locked on mine while her wolf crawled through them.

"What happened?" She coughed softly, tried again. "You were hurt, I could feel it, but I couldn't get to you and they wouldn't let me go—" Hysteria rose in her voice until I sent her power, soothed her with magic.

"Batsheva won the first round," I said. "I'm up for a rematch."

Charlotte quivered as I rose from the bed and headed to the door.

"Well?" I grinned at her, turning back. "Are you coming or not?"

Silly question.

Chapter Thirty Four

I thought I was ready for anything. Sebastian and Sunny quickly filled me in as I arrived in the kitchen, that a battle had been fought and was now at a standoff at Batsheva's castle. Pannera had her surrounded, while Enforcers, at least according to Mom's intel, kept the war zone contained. It was clear Pannera wasn't about to allow Batsheva to keep the essence, though I was a little confused. Now that she had my vampire, why wasn't Batsheva able to defeat Pannera?

There could only be one answer. And it gave me more hope than I probably should have had.

We traveled together, a string of witches, vampires, a demon cat and one werewolf girl as I tore the veil open and pulled them through with me. The rubbery membrane welcomed me home, but the extra draw of it was lost thanks to all of the people I had with me. I'd never attempted to transport so many before, but no way was I waiting around because someone couldn't find a ride.

All or nothing.

The veil slit open, emptying us out into the corridor outside the throne room. I could feel the hum of magic outside, the pressure of the Enforcer shielding and welcomed it. Their attention meant no one would be escaping until I was ready to deal with them.

Margaret was going to be so mad at me for using her tactics against her.

Couldn't wait for that confrontation.

Mom marched beside me, Gram slightly behind, Sassafras scampering between my feet and through the door before I reached it, demon magic preceding me as he let loose a wall of fire.

Good thing, too. The gathered vampires probably wouldn't have even noticed we were there if he hadn't put on such a show. As it was, it looked like I'd arrived just in time.

Not to stop a war. I couldn't have cared less about their petty squabbles at the moment. But to keep Pannera from killing Batsheva before I got the chance.

They both spun, Sebastian's Queen dressed in tight black leather, ball gown long gone, her cascading hair bound in a thick braid wound around her shoulders like a shawl. Batsheva was in full vampire mode, though her humanity returned as she glared at me as every vampire in the room, all poised for death and destruction, stopped and turned to see me storm in.

With my own little army at my back.

Just try and take us on.

"You!" Batsheva jabbed a long, pointed claw at me, eyes burning white. "You were meant to die!"

"Better luck next time." I stopped in front of them, my power pushing the other vampires back as Mom, Gram and I faced them down. I could feel Meira behind me, Sassafras joining her, Sebastian, Sunny and Uncle Frank sealing up the end of the line.

Pannera pulled back, but I knew she wasn't going to stand down easily.

"How did you survive?" Was that real curiosity in her eyes? Respect even?

Who cared?

"I'm here to take her back." I pointed at Batsheva's chest, knowing my vampire would be lodged there. "We can do this easy or we can do it so hard you'll never recover. Your decision."

Batsheva snarled and threw a thick bolt of lightning at me, spirit magic sizzling. Shaylee had already grounded us firmly to the earth while my demon slashed at the attack, family magic absorbing it with a happy surge of power.

"Nice try." I snapped my fingers, fire crackling, and slammed her with a fist of demon power. The fire just set her fancy suit coat alight, sending her scrambling backward, shrieking and slapping at the curling smoke and embers.

"This is not permitted!" Batsheva turned to Pannera, soot covering one hand, white frill at her throat now crisped and black. Seeing no support from her rival, she spit at me. "Treaty rules," she said. "Attacking a clan Queen is punishable by death."

"You tried that already," I said. "Feel like coming up with a better plan? Because your first one seems to have a pretty big flaw." I turned to Mom with a perky smile. "Suggestions, Council Leader?"

Mom's answering grin was tight and full of the desire to hurt someone. In particular. "Kill the bitch," she said. "Any way you can."

I spun back to Batsheva who finally seemed nervous, bless her evil, black, twisted little heart, while my family fanned out and raised shields of their own as the gathered vampires threatened. Knowing my back was firmly covered, I found myself smiling. "Well, then," I said. "Sounds like it's my turn." I raised my hand, eyes drifting to Celeste who was looking decidedly panicked and ticked off one finger. "For betraying all magic users on our plane to the Brotherhood of sorcerers, I sentence you to death."

Both clans muttered, Pannera's eyes empty. A handful of vampires tried to rush me, but Meira sent them packing with a whip of flames she wielded with expert ease. All that fighting on Demonicon did wonders for her talent.

My second finger fell. "For using sorcery to undermine Yvette Wilhelm and win over her clan, I sentence you to death."

More muttering. Angry now. But only on her side and now turned away from us and internalized. Demetrius poked his head out from behind the throne and bobbed it at me. Good, he was here. I was going to need what he carried if my plan was going to work.

"For cheating with sorcery in the battle against Yvette Wilhelm, draining her power with illegal magic, I sentence you to death." My last finger dropped and I aimed the index at Celeste. "You're next."

I'm sure she got the irony.

Uproar followed my words, on both sides again, though Pannera remained as she had before, still and blank.

"You have no proof!" Batsheva was in major meltdown mode. Her face flickered from vampire to human, some of her perfection lost, the old her peeking through at times, the dumpy, wrinkled woman she used to be, as though the power inside her rejected her completely.

I was counting on it.

I gestured to Demetrius who crept forward, skirting

her to come to my side and hunch at my feet. "Tell them."

He did. Without a trace of crazy. And better yet, he showed them. More amazing than any big screen event, Demetrius drew from the power around him to cast a three dimensional holographic show for all to witness.

From Batsheva bowing to the Brotherhood, Demetrius among them, to her using a crystal to influence others, through the battle she fought with Yvette, that same crystal stealing the magic of the Queen until she fell, weakened and helpless.

To my downfall. It was hard to watch, seeing her hover over me. I could almost feel her teeth in my neck again, rubbing at it absently as the scene played out. My disappearance through the veil.

Batsheva's battle with the essence as my vampire tried to free herself.

Yes. So I was right after all.

The air around us went dark again, show over. But not one entity present resented Demetrius's borrowing of power, nor did they doubt for a moment what he'd shown was the truth.

Gotcha.

"Clearly we have all been deceived." Pannera turned to Batsheva who practically frothed at the mouth. "I agree with Coven Leader Hayle's pronouncement and sentence you to death."

Batsheva's clan roared, but not to support her, their rage pushing against her as she spun on them and snarled. "Stop!" The shriek reached them all, froze them in their tracks.

Punched me in the stomach. I felt it too. She still had power over me.

It was the best thing I'd learned all night.

"Batsheva," I stepped forward, "I challenge you for leadership of this clan."

Power flashed over my head as Margaret and Elliot finally made an appearance. Ruining my moment, damn them. I scowled at the Council Leader as she landed with a thud between the vampires and me, face a round, red, wrinkled apple of absolute rage.

"What the hell are you doing?" She stomped one foot, hands in fists waving around her. "Are you out of your mind?"

Mom was already moving, her own fury radiating, but I stopped her before she could clothesline the woman with a snap of magic. "I stake claim to this clan," I said. "I have the right." I pointed at Margaret as she struggled to breathe. "A right you insisted on."

Take that and choke on it.

She finally caught air, body vibrating with the need to hurt me. Let her try. I'd already been drained of blood and part of my soul, dumped in the veil and left for dead. Nothing she could bring would compare to that.

"Very well." Um, really? "Finish this." She turned away from me, hands still clutched tightly together while Batsheva spluttered.

"She has no rights here."

"I do," I said. "I felt your command. You made me part of your clan. And now I am challenging you. Yes, or no?" I grinned, unable to help myself. "Unless you're afraid of me."

I reached for my vampire in the same moment, praying what I was about to do would work. Drove my magic inside Batsheva, searching, calling.

And my vampire answered.

She pulled partially free from the Queen, the shining white mass of her yearning toward me. Only for a moment, until she snapped back inside Batsheva, but it was enough. For me, knowing she was in there, autonomous, whole, but for the rest of the gathering as well.

"She doesn't want to be with you," I said. "And I'm taking her back."

Batsheva spun on Margaret one more time. "This is your territory," she said, desperation finally rising. "Will you allow other magic users to come into your house and break your laws?"

"Like you did? You made Sydlynn Hayle part of your clan. She is within her rights." Margaret fell cold. She waved one hand, fury gone, face tired, but angry. "Accept the challenge or I'll deal with you personally. And so help me heaven," she spun on her heel, turning in a slow circle, before coming to face Pannera, "you lot will abide by what happens and if I hear one more breath of trouble from you, I'm wiping you all out. Personally."

Nice to know frustration finally forced her to do what was right.

I drew a breath to thank her just as Batsheva flung herself at me.

Chapter Thirty Five

I slammed up a ring of demon shielding around the pair of us to keep her from attacking my family and dove right at her.

Yeah, I was ready. She wasn't exactly hard to read.

Instead of attacking her directly, I let my vampire do it. Called to her as I had before, this time ready to grab onto her as she emerged.

Batsheva fell as I dodged, landing on all fours, turning to roar, glowing with the magic of the clan. But she doubled over when she tried to rise, my vampire pulling free again, leaning toward me as I reached with the spirit magic of the Hayle family and connected with her.

Only for a moment before Batsheva stuffed her down again. But enough I knew this was going to work.

Over and over Batsheva struck at me, while over and over I called out the essence to come back to me. Panting and sobbing her rage, the Queen finally collapsed to the ground, writhing as the clan power fought against the essence of the vampires for control. I let the shielding drop and turned to Demetrius who stood and tossed something shining toward me. The crystal landed in my hand as if magicked there, the power of it pulsing with my vampire's energy.

The essence she'd filled it with. Time to end this. For the last time I called her.

She rose from Batsheva who shrieked her denial, but drawing on the energy she'd stored in the crystal, amplified by the sorcery I had at my command, the essence stepped outside of Batsheva's body, her spirit body snapping with a loud crack as she severed the connection.

I turned the hungry crystal on Batsheva, drawing out the clan magic, trapping it in the stone, feeling it flood with power and the life force controlling the clan as Batsheva withered and aged, her body shrinking, deflating, until she was a wrinkled old woman, arms and legs flailing around her.

"My clan," I said with great satisfaction, "drain her."

They hardly needed the invitation. Her screaming faded to a whisper and then to silence until they backed away, wiping lips wet with blood, the mummified form of their former leader staring up at me.

As I'd looked. Only she wasn't invincible.

"Wrap her in rags," I said. "Make sure she can't escape." I looked up and met her eyes, my vampire, the essence.

She glowed perfectly white, though bits of red and gray clung to her edges. I remembered Trill's warning and opened my power to her. "You're in pain."

"I am free," she said, voice a song, welcoming my help as the bits burned away in sparks of sparkling light until she was once again clean, untainted. "And I am grateful."

She turned and faced the vampires, Margaret who had joined Mom and the family, Pannera. The essence raised her arms as though to embrace us all before speaking.

"We must prepare for war," she said. "The Brotherhood connives to turn us against one another while the ones who can save us struggle alone. It is time to work together, to set aside petty grievances and old rules that no longer serve a purpose." Nice gut shot at Margaret and the whole vampire system. Looked like it hit right on target. "The time is coming when we either stand together, or fall alone. That is a choice you each must make." She turned back to me, her female shape sharpening as she focused, and I found myself smiling.

She looked like me.

"I've made my choice already," she said, drifting toward me. "I choose Sydlynn Hayle. I just hope you're all as foresighted."

No one protested, not even Pannera. Good thing. Wouldn't have done her any good.

Heart aching and full of longing, I opened my arms and welcomed my vampire home.

Chapter Thirty Six

Funny to find myself in my old quarters again, sitting on a chair, looking out the window, waiting for the party to start. Only this time I was the one calling the shots.

I just wished I could promise everyone a happy ending.

A short detour on my way to my room, while Piotr was ordered to call on all of the clan leaders to come to be adopted by their new Queen, had me standing in front of the portrait I'd seen earlier. The one that broke my heart. Charlotte hovered behind me, face expressionless as I stared up at the face I knew so well, wishing there was another way to end this conflict once and for all.

But there wasn't. And sacrifices had to be made. Though I really hoped I wasn't ruining something truly amazing because I had to have support against the Brotherhood.

Responsibility sucked sometimes.

The family waited for me in my old room after I turned down Batsheva's Queenly quarters with disgust. No way was I letting her smarm rub off even an iota more than it already had. Margaret and Elliot hovering to one side, when I returned. This time I didn't mind hugging my mother in front of the other leader. I think we'd shown just how strong we were, thanks. Gram was next, Meira after her. Sassafras's purr rattled my teeth. My vampire friends were missing, presumably thanks to Pannera, though Uncle Frank stood with Mom, a grim smile on his face.

"Good job, kiddo," he said.

"Thanks, Uncle Frank." I grinned back. Sighed. Turned to Margaret. "I had no intention of breaking your laws. But I couldn't let Batsheva have the essence."

Speaking of whom, the essence hugged me for the gazillionth time deep inside, the most affectionate I'd ever known her, as Margaret spoke. I almost missed what the woman said because I was busy hugging my vampire back while my demon clamped herself around us, Shaylee pulled in too while the family magic cocooned us nice and tight.

Happy family? Check.

"I'm just glad it worked out." Margaret shook her head, sinking to a chair, face pale. "I don't know why I sided with them, Miriam. What was I thinking?"

Uh-oh. I reached for her, but not before Demetrius went sniffing. Turned to me with his blue eyes full of anger.

"Coerced," he said.

The Brotherhood.

Of course she didn't want to believe it. But it only took a moment, and a gentle squeeze of her shoulder from the very kindly Elliot who whispered, "You really haven't been yourself, my dear," for Margaret Applegate to finally admit the truth.

That and a sudden attack by Demetrius Strong. At least, that was what it looked like to me, and Elliot from the look on the Enforcer's face. But Demetrius didn't harm Margaret.

Just grabbed her hand and pulled.

The portly European Leader cried out and jerked free of him, one of her fingers suddenly red as her eyes flew wide, mouth dropping open. The former leader of the Chosen of the Light held up his hand, a gold ring balanced in his palm.

"You see," he said. "Trust me now, yes, yes, trust me forever."

"Oh my very word," Margaret whispered, staring at the ring while Mom gasped softly, her hand going to her throat. Margaret enveloped the item in a ball of blue light, pulling it slowly toward her, face very pale before she let it hover before her eyes. When hers met mine, I knew it, felt her freedom, understood Demetrius was absolutely right.

She'd been manipulated and controlled by the sorcerers.

And man, was she pissed about it.

After a flurry of, "Arrogant, black-hearted, conniving... I'll get to the bottom of this, mark my words," she stormed out with Elliot in tow, crackling with magic and calling for her Enforcers. Mom smiled at me, tired around her eyes, but clearly pleased from the sparkle in her gaze.

"I pity the Brotherhood members she uncovers," Mom said, though her worry was clear and I knew what she was thinking.

If the European Council Leader was under influence, was our territory safe? I could tell Mom would be doing a thorough investigation the moment she got back, if I correctly read the intense, growing anger on her face.

I turned to Demetrius who was now carefully examining his belly button lint and humming. "Well done."

He ignored me, petting the little patch of fuzz he dug out of his navel.

Ew.

I wandered to the corner to be alone while the others gathered to talk. Put up a wall around me so they knew to leave me be. And while I probably should have let them in, even Charlotte held outside the circle of privacy I erected, I really just needed to be alone to think.

Could I do it? Break up a family because of duty and necessity? Could I break hearts I loved because of the maji and the Brotherhood?

I had no choice.

It wasn't long before Piotr entered and bowed to me, eyes going to the crystal full of power in my lap.

"The leaders of your clan have gathered," he said. "My Queen."

I rose and went after him, Gram hooking one arm through mine as we made our way back to the throne room.

Pannera was still there, only her side was greatly reduced in number, only a handful of vampires with her.

"If I might remain," she said, eyes narrowed.

"I have nothing to hide," I said. Turned my back on her. Walked the length of the carpet to the throne.

I turned as if to sit, caught the flare of fury in Pannera's eyes and addressed the room.

"I was made a member of this clan by your last Queen, Batsheva." My eyes scanned the crowd and, for the first time, I found myself swearing internally. I'd forgotten someone very important in the whole mess with Batsheva.

Celeste was nowhere to be seen.

Damn it.

No time to deal with her now. I had to finish this before Pannera started another war.

"I fought her, defeated her with her own power. And drained her magic, the magic of the clan." Yeah, I'd cheated too. Used sorcery to do it. But none of the gathered vampires seemed to know or even care. They stared up at me with a mix of hope and anger, awe and fear.

"There is one problem," I said. "Though I possess the clan's power, I can't lead you." I held out the crystal pulsing with contained magic. "I have other responsibilities, a coven to protect. And I know you will never accept me as your own unless I become a true vampire. Which I can't do." A mutter of agreement, less anger, more curiosity.

"You have been hurt by this conflict," I said. "This family has been broken and damaged by lies and deceit. You need strong leadership, someone you trust to take you forward."

Piotr actually had the balls to step toward me. I had to hand it to him, he was pretty full of himself. Even Pannera's eyebrows shot up as he held out his hand.

"Queens have ruled for centuries," he said with a smile. "Perhaps it is time for a King's leadership."

Like hell. I struck him with a fist of spirit magic, sending him flying backward to crash to the floor as his fellow vampires scattered to let him fall.

"I have no proof you were involved or had knowledge of Batsheva's treachery," I said, "but I don't think I'm the only one in this clan who will never, ever trust you."

They snarled at him, power curling around them as they glared.

Piotr took the hint.

"No," I said, "there is only one vampire to lead this clan. Only one who can repair the trust and create a strong, healthy family worthy of your name." I caught Sunny's eyes, saw the dawning understanding in her face as I held out my hand to her.

"Teresa Wilhelm," I said, calling her by her real name, the one etched under her portrait, hanging by Yvette, "come and claim your throne."

Chapter Thirty Seven

Sunny didn't hesitate, crossing the carpet to ascend to my side while I kept an eye on Pannera. But the opposing Queen didn't argue so even she must have known this was the only way to end the conflict.

Sunny ignored my outstretched hand and the power there, instead staring into my eyes for a long moment.

A little warning might have been nice. She softened the chastisement with a mental caress. *How long have you known?*

That you're a Wilhelm? I shrugged. *You transfer very well to paint.*

The damned portrait. Her blue eyes sparkled. *Yvette insisted.*

You're her sister? Daughter?

No, just a descendant. Sunny hugged me to her, lips pressed to my cheek. *We have more in common than you think,*

Syd. You're not the only one who's run from who she's meant to be.

Is this okay? I held out the crystal again. *You went to all that trouble of cleaning your blood of the Wilhelm family. Do you need to do it again to take over?*

No, she sent. *Just the power. No amount of orders from Pannera can come between me and the full magic of being Queen.*

When we parted, we were both smiling.

Until Piotr spoke up.

"She is no longer a member of our family." His snarl of rage surprised me, though it shouldn't have. "Abandoned her Queen, her clan. I refuse to accept her as my ruler."

"Oh, shut up," I said. "Or I'll silence you myself."

Sunny held one hand up, palm flat. "I accept," she said. *My past has caught up to me. But I'm all right with it.*

Sunny. I hesitated. *I'm sorry. I really am.* I glanced at Uncle Frank. On the other side. Pannera's vampire.

Don't be. Her fingers twitched. *You're right, I'm the only choice. Now hand it over so you can go home.*

Not we.

What had I done?

The crystal was heavy in my hand as I turned it over and pressed it to hers. My vampire acted immediately, urging out the power. But it needed little encouragement, flowing from the crystal and into Sunny in a rush, as if it had been waiting for her forever. Sunny straightened, eyes flaring with magic, whole body glowing with pure white light until it faded, the transfer complete.

Turning with great grace, she settled into her throne with one smooth movement to the sound of cheering from her clan.

What followed was familiar, the adoption ceremony repeated dozens of times as the leaders of her clan came forward to accept her blood and have theirs accepted in return, leaving her then to retreat to their own clans to share her blood with their people. I left her to her work, going to Mom's side, unable to look up, keeping my eyes on the carpet, hands clenched around the crystal.

I could feel a fraction of the clan magic still inside it, knew I'd carry it with me forever now. Just another layer in an already complicated Syd.

The worst? Sunny without Uncle Frank. It just wasn't fair.

A strong hand settled on my shoulder as the last of Sunny's people retreated, her fingers delicately wiping at the blood on her lips. Uncle Frank stepped past me, turning to face Sebastian.

"I ask to be released from my blood oath to your clan," he said.

My heart clenched. This was my big worry, the fear I carried. He had to do what Sunny had done when she joined Sebastian's family after the run-in with Nicholas—drain his blood to the point of no return, be filled again by his new clan. While she made light of it, I knew it was painful and probably very dangerous.

If Sunny lost Uncle Frank because of this, she'd never forgive me. And I'd never forgive myself.

Sebastian looked sad a moment, but nodded. "I am willing to release you," he said as his eyes went to Pannera.

Hang on. Was it that easy? Did I worry myself for nothing? Could she just let him go?

That would be wicked.

My stirring excitement faded the moment I saw the look on her face.

And drove me to dive into her mind even as she was opening her mouth.

Don't even think about saying no, I snarled. *I swear to you, if you don't let him go to be with Sunny, I'll hunt you down in your little castle and pull it down around your ears.*

She glared at me, lips parted.

I look forward to it, she sent.

"Considering the circumstances," Pannera said out loud, "and as a show of good faith to my new counterpart," she gave Sunny the barest of nods, "I agree to release Frank Hayle from my clan so he may join his true love." If there was more honey in her tone, we all would have died of diabetic shock.

Instead, she raised one hand, white spirit magic striking outward to plunge into Uncle Frank. He cried out, grasped his chest, falling to his knees as sparks flew from his body, cascading to the floor while he doubled over into a crouch, the last of the clan magic flying free.

I almost moved to help him, but he didn't need me. Slowly, in obvious pain, he forced himself to stand, to walk forward a pace. Another. Until he fell to his knees at Sunny's feet.

"My love," he whispered, the sound carrying in the total silence of the room, "I would be a part of you forever."

She slid one hand under his chin, tipped his head back, bent over him. Her lips touched his, the kiss deep and passionate and when they parted, there was blood on both their lips.

"Welcome, my love," she said. "My Prince."

I would have clapped and squealed like a little girl if I didn't have dignity to uphold.

I've given you what you want, Pannera sent, dulling my joy with the jab of magic accompanying her words. *Now stay out of my way*.

I didn't have a chance to answer, not while Sunny beckoned to me. I approached, smiling at the happy couple, as they beamed back.

"I thought I screwed everything up." Tears sprang in my eyes. "I'm so happy for you."

Sunny took my hand, Uncle Frank bending to kiss my cheek as the new Queen of the Wilhelm Clan bit the soft flesh of my wrist and tasted my blood before offering the tip of her finger and the bead of blood standing there. I drank, not freaked or grossed out this time, the flavor of her blood full of sparks and flowers.

"Sydlynn Hayle," she said, "you will always be a part of this clan. And you will always be welcome."

Chapter Thirty Eight

My first impulse, once I strode triumphant from the throne room, was to dash for the nearest exit, run for home, lock myself in my room and scrub the last several days from my memory forever.

Elliot didn't give me the chance, waiting for me right at the exit. He was lucky he was an Enforcer or I would have done him some damage.

"A moment yet," he said. "My leader would like a word?"

Oh, so now she wanted to talk to me, did she? I stomped my way to my old quarters, remembering I had something to retrieve anyway, so it was a good thing after all. No way was I leaving the magic blocking powder for some conniving vampire to find when I had my own plans for it.

Just wait until I saw Ameline again. One deep breath

and it would all be over.

I brought Mom and Gram with me anyway, just in case. No way was Margaret putting me in magical irons and dragging me off to trial. Not without a fight.

But this Margaret, the one who stopped pacing as we entered, she was far different from the woman I'd first met. She was still pale, deflated, a balloon without her air.

"It's horrible," she said immediately on our arrival. "There are Brotherhood everywhere in my territory."

A short, babbling explanation later gave us the full picture. "Three covens now under control of the sorcerers. Two of those coven's Council Members also. And the Enforcers." She fluttered a hand over her chest. "Elliot is beside himself. It didn't take much examination to uncover the truth. Over half of our Enforcers have ties to the Brotherhood."

Mom took her hand, led her to a sofa and sat her down. "I'm happy to help any way I can."

Margaret nodded quickly, some of her spunk returning. "When I think I, myself, was under their control, even that little bit. And all because of this." She held up the ring Demetrius freed her from still surrounded by a blue force shield. "I lost my favorite and Elliot replaced it for me." She tossed it to me. "Feel it."

I knew before she shed the shield and it dropped in my hand the small diamond embedded in it was part of a power crystal. "How long have you had it?"

"Not long," she said, anger rising. "Just a month or so. But long enough. I've been a fool."

"No," Mom said. "How were you to know?"

Margaret didn't have an answer for that.

"Their power is insidious," Mom said. "I'm amazed you uncovered what you did so quickly."

Margaret's lips thinned to a grim line. "Amazing what you can find when you know what you're looking for." She sighed then, met my eyes. "I'm sorry, Coven Leader," she said. "The European Council stands at the ready to assist in the fight against the Brotherhood." She paused. "When we've finished cleaning our house, that is."

After a brief goodbye, the door closed behind her as she hurried off to do just that.

Gram's arm slid around my shoulders. "Well done, girl." She smacked me firmly with a kiss on the cheek. "Well done."

Mom rose, came to us. Hugged us both. "I was so worried," she whispered. "But you have made me so proud, sweetheart." Her face hardened, but not at me. "I hope I can count on you, Coven Leader, when I go looking for the thieves in our midst?"

Deep breath. Prepare for the worst. "Though you know I'm one too, right?

Mom went pale but Gram didn't react, watching, eyes narrowed.

"Syd," Mom whispered. "What are you talking

about?"

I filled her in on what Demetrius said. "I'm part sorcerer too, Mom." I felt like hugging myself but stayed still, solid, as if I knew what I was doing. "It's necessary. For my evolution." Eye-rolling happened without my permission and I heard Gram giggle.

"We'll just keep this to ourselves, will we?" She poked me firmly in the ribs. "I trust you're not under the Brotherhood's influence?"

Mom nodded slowly. "Syd," she said, "you can't tell anyone." A thin thread of panic reached me from her. "Not anyone. Promise me."

"Trust me," I said. "It's not something I want to spread around. I'm already under enough scrutiny thanks to the gang." My index finger tapped against my temple. "I get it. But yes," I winked at Gram, "you can be assured the Brotherhood and I are on opposite sides."

Was I really that sure?

Not going there.

Mom hugged me quickly. "You amaze me," she whispered. "You're so much stronger than I ever was."

Wow. Choke. Tear time at last?

Not quite. Not yet.

"Your pardon." I pulled free of my happy mother and grandmother to find Sebastian standing at the door. "My Queen would like a word with you."

I'd heard that before.

"Like hell." Mom actually planted herself in front of me while Gram stalked forward and got into his face.

"Tell that thing you answer to," she jabbed him in the chest with one pointy finger, standing on her tiptoes, fuzzy socks now filthy, "she can bloody well stay away from my granddaughter."

The door eased open further as Pannera let herself in.

"Tell me yourself," she said, not having any idea who she was trying to push around.

"Come in," I said, blocking Gram just before she did something nasty and probably deadly to the vampire Queen, knowing Sebastian would be devastated if I let Gram kill her. "It's all right, Gram."

My grandmother backed off, faded blue eyes slits of anger as she followed the Queen's progress further into the room.

"I understand our Council Leader has uncovered uncomfortable truths." Pannera's statue features remained as rock-hard as ever.

"The Brotherhood are coming," I said. "You heard what my vampire told everyone." My vampire. That was right. The flash of anger Pannera let out just made me smile.

Suck it up, buttercup.

My vampire. So there.

"I did hear," she said. "And understood. And with the present news of the Brotherhood's infiltration of the witch network, I am now inclined to examine my own family for such intrusions."

"Probably a good idea," I said.

"Do not for a moment think you and I are friends or allies in any way." Pannera turned and headed for the door, tone mile as though discussing the weather. "But you kept your part of our bargain. Which means you at least have some sense of honor."

Oh, seriously. Like she was one to talk.

Pannera stopped at my door, gaze lost out the window at the mountains etched against the night sky. "When you need help against the sorcerers," she said, "my clan will answer your call."

Sebastian bowed his way out after her, eyes locked on mine, a small smile on his face.

I won.

Imagine that.

Chapter Thirty Nine

I shuffled nervously at the bottom of the stairs, pulling at the spaghetti strap on my right shoulder as it slipped down over my bare arm. The flowers clutched in my hands looked pretty on the surface, but the bundled stems had long begun to brown from the fidgeting and sweat of my anxious hands.

Meira looked over her shoulder and winked at me, her matching dress perfect on her figure. My sister had a figure. Growing up way too fast for my liking.

"Stop," she whispered. "You'll wrinkle."

Sunny had to pick pink silk, didn't she? Bad enough it skimmed my body so close wearing underwear was a questionable activity, the sticky bra thingies she forced me to slap on driving me nuts. The shoes were another story altogether, so high they rivaled anything Pagomaris, my demon grandmother's aide, forced me to wear on

Demonicon. Sure, they made my butt look good, but the balls of my feet were killing me.

And pink? Pink?

Oh. My. Swearword.

Don't get me wrong, I was honored she and Uncle Frank still wanted me to stand with them. They'd failed to mention Sebastian was their best man. Not like it was a problem. But now I was back home, back to my normal not-so-normal, remembering how he'd kissed me, the dream I'd had... let's just say I was feeling a little awkward about the whole situation.

Gracious as ever, if he felt awkward as well he didn't show it, though I noticed he did do his best to keep his distance, so maybe he was just better at hiding it.

I looked up as Sunny swept down the stairs, Mom behind her, the pair of them beaming in delight. Sunny looked absolutely stunning in her pure white gown, as flowing and silky as the one I wore. Except she made me look like I was wearing a burlap sack.

Gorgeous.

She kissed first me, then Meira, her lips soft and a little sticky with lipstick. Giggling, she wiped at our cheeks before smiling at Mom.

"Thank you, Miriam," she said.

"We love you so much." Mom hugged her before sliding into her black robe. "Are you ready?"

My feet just wanted to get it over with.

There had been protest from her new clan, that the wedding be held at the castle, but Sunny was adamant. "My family, my rules," she said. The wedding would go, as planned, in my back yard, the happy couple surrounded by those who loved them, no matter the clan affiliation or magic race.

Though Sunny confessed with a wicked laugh, the real vampire bonding ceremony would happen later. When she and Uncle Frank were alone together.

Just TMI.

I peeked out the back door, spotted Uncle Frank at the far end of the lawn, Mom joining him, Liam standing by in his own tuxedo. I'd been surprised when my uncle asked Liam to be his second usher, but it wasn't like I kept tabs on my family or how close Uncle Frank had grown to my Sidhe friend.

Them getting along, being buddies, kind of appealed to me.

I let my eyes land on Sebastian a moment before flickering away again. Drew a shaky breath.

Sunny giggled, looking so young and sweet and stunningly beautiful I had to giggle with her.

"I'm the one who's supposed to be nervous." She wrinkled her nose. Looked suddenly anxious. "Do I look all right?"

File that with one of the stupidest questions ever asked ever. Meira gushed all over her immediately.

"You look so beautiful I can't stand it, Aunt Sunny," she said.

Sunny flushed. Kissed her cheek again. "Thank you," she whispered. "I like the sound of that."

Music sounded as Mom turned to face us. The lovely strains of a classical piece. Leave it to Sunny to turn up her nose at the traditional march. Meira winked at us both before squaring her shoulders and tottering down the hall to the stretch of red carpet Sunny purchased for the aisle. I watched her go, a moment of sadness overcoming me. Time had passed, so much of it, with so much more to go. Sunny leaned in to me as I dabbed at a tear while my sister, the baby she was long gone, took measured steps down the carpet past happy guests oohing and ahhing over her dress.

"I love you," Sunny whispered. I turned and hugged her, wrinkles and mussed hair be damned as she clung to me.

"I love you so much, Sunny." I let her go, a little breathless, tears in my eyes, laughing and trying not to cry. "I guess I better go, huh?"

It was a long, long walk with all those eyes on me, but a happy one. I couldn't wipe the smile from my face, broke convention to hug Uncle Frank who pulled me tightly against him, cheek on my hair.

"She's perfect for us," I said.

He laughed. "She really is." His eyes lifted, attention

shifting immediately and I stepped into my place to turn and watch my friend become my aunt.

I thought she was beautiful in the hallway. Under the light of the moon and the twinkling white lights and pale gauze decorating the back yard, Sunny appeared from the house like a glowing goddess. Her blonde hair cascaded over one shoulder, blue eyes framed by stunning black lashes, dress floating around her and the single white lily she carried. I'd laughed at her choice, the flower of death, but she'd been right about one thing.

It went perfectly with her dress.

No one said anything, just smiled and smiled as she progressed down the aisle to join us. Uncle Frank was long lost, her too, and even I struggled to keep up when Mom began the ceremony. In fact, I have no idea how she did it. I wouldn't have been able to focus.

In a lovely blend of vampire and witch, mixed with a healthy dose of traditional wedding designed by Sunny and Uncle Frank, two of the people I loved most in the world joined hands, hearts and souls for all eternity.

Tear time had finally arrived.

Why was I not surprised Sunny kept the best part of a human ceremony? As Mom pronounced them married, she smiled. "You may kiss your bride."

Not like Uncle Frank needed the encouragement.

Sashenka pulled me aside the moment I was free, hugging me and gushing over my dress. "I'm so happy

Sunny invited me," she said. "It was really lovely of her."

"I know." I turned and watched as the pair laughed with a group of witches, the perfect, flawless, movie-star couple. "She's awesome."

"I know this might be bad timing." Sashenka grasped my hand and led me to the corner of the yard while Mom and Gram orchestrated a magical transformation, turning the seating area into a dance floor and buffet dining, food appearing from nowhere—the family's kitchens, they'd been cooking all day—to fill the tables.

"Trust me," I said. "I've had a hell of a week. Just hit me."

She laughed. "It's nothing bad," she said. "At least, I hope you don't think so." She drew a breath and blurted on. "I've been thinking about what we talked about. And I'd like to join the Hayle coven."

Wow. "You would?"

"If you want me." She dimpled, blushed. "You don't have to make me your second or anything, but I'd do a great job if you did, I promise. I've had lots of experience."

"Have you talked to Tallah?" Wow. Did I say wow?

"Not yet." Sashenka's face fell a little. "But if you want to move forward, I will." She waited, every emotion showing on her face. "No rush or anything."

I laughed and hugged her. "We'll talk to your sister," I said. "Together."

And hope doing so didn't ruin a loving family.

Food and laughter and a half a glass of champagne later and I felt overwhelmed. Uncle Frank had always promised to take me out in the middle of nowhere and get me drunk when I turned eighteen, just to see what would happen. Most witches didn't deal well with alcohol, and considering my particular situation, with my luck I'd total something large and necessary.

We never had the chance. Made me sad to think about it. Liam appeared at my side while Sashenka was off dancing with a handsome vampire and swept me to the dance floor myself.

"No looking sad on such an amazing night." He smiled down at me, Sidhe power sliding around me like a hug.

"Sorry," I said, hiccupped. "Time just goes by so fast."

Liam leaned down and kissed me. Without hesitation, without his normal feeling of waiting for me to reject him. He just kissed me and let me feel his heart through his magic before laughing as his lips set me free.

"Good thing you have lots of it then," he said.

Smartass.

Uncle Frank liberated me from Liam after a few dances in which I was actually really starting to have a good time. My handsome uncle spun me in circles to a pop tune, and only then did I realize what a great dancer he was.

"Thank you for loving me," I said, tears coming again. "For always having my back."

He swept me up, spun me around, lips on my ear.

"Syd," he whispered. "What are favorite uncles for?" He set me down, bowed over my hand as a slow song started. But before we could go on, Sebastian stepped up and took his place, Sunny at his side.

"Shall we exchange partners?" Sebastian handed Sunny off to her husband—more tears—and watched as the happy pair joined together and danced away as though floating above the ground.

I offered my hand, sliding it over the smooth, cool skin of Sebastian's palm and let him lead.

"I want to thank you," he said. "The clans are no longer at each other's throats. There is hope for real peace between us."

"Nice to know." I caught Liam watching, saw his jealousy and actually grinned at him until he ducked his head and blushed.

"We need to talk." Sebastian's tone was light, but he lowered his voice as he spoke. "About how I feel for you."

That was unexpected. And totally floored me.

"Okay," I said like a total idiot.

He smiled, humor lighting his eyes. He really was absolutely delicious. "The first time I bit you, to save you from the sorcerer's powder, I felt it." Sebastian shuddered just a little, hunger rising in those laughing eyes. "The connection between us. When I did , some of your spirit returned to me. Linking us together."

I seemed to have that effect on people. "I'm sorry," I said.

"Don't be." He sighed. "At first, I was merely curious. But when the vampire essence took over, when death called to me with so powerful a voice, it was you who saved me."

"Me?" I would have stopped dancing, but he had a firm grip and kept us moving. "Why me?"

"That part of your spirit, it kept me sane, at least sane enough to retreat to the cave and hide so I wouldn't harm anyone." His head lowered, lips next to my temple, heat rising between us. "When you rescued me from my perpetual death, I tried to tell myself it was only gratitude that led me to kiss you. But I know better."

Oh boy. I wasn't sure I was ready for this blurting of feelings from him. But he was still calm, casual, as though he needed to speak it, even if nothing happened after.

"When you absorbed the essence, became vampire, the pull became stronger yet." His fingers tightened on my back but his movements never wavered. "And with the second bite, since you asked me to free you a second time, I must confess, I'm finding you rather irresistible."

Well now. Everything else went away in a rush as the

passion in his eyes flared and threatened to devour me. And I was more than willing to let that happen.

"You have shaken me to my core, when I thought no one could touch me," he said. "Not after all these years. And though I have sworn to remain alone forever, I'm finding it a pity you are part of another clan."

"Clan loyalties can change," I said without thinking. "And forever is a long time to be alone."

Sebastian gently released me as the song ended, shattering the spell holding us together. He bent over my hand, kissed it gently, a spark of spirit passing between us.

"Indeed," he said. "Thank you for the dance."

As I watched him go, I hovered between giggling and blushing though I knew now, no matter what happened, how long I lived, if I chose to pursue it, the future always had possibilities.

Chapter Forty

Happy ending? Well, kinda.

Trill and Owen and their Nona were long gone when we returned from Austria, though I wasn't surprised. At least I knew they were doing well and, if Trill's attitude was any indication, moving ahead with gathering the maji army.

At least, I hoped that's what it meant. Because after the run-in I'd had with the Brotherhood, knowing now how deeply they were entrenched in Europe, it felt like we were very quickly running out of time.

Quaid was slightly startled when I reached out to him and thanked him for watching over the Zornovs. Even said "You're welcome," without snark. We were okay then.

Good info to have. Because, honestly, it was hard to know with him sometimes.

I brought home the mummified form of Batsheva, with full intentions of putting her crazy ass out in the sun. But one look in her eyes took me back to the cave and Sebastian, to my own suffering. So, instead, I dragged her down to the basement, stuffed her in a corner.

And forgot about her.

Don't judge me. Served her right.

There was no sign of Ameline, though I was hardly surprised. She clearly had her own agenda, but at least she said she was as opposed to the Brotherhood as I was. If for the wrong reasons, enough to make me worry all over again. And though she'd technically given me what I needed to escape, I was not falling down the hole of "thank yous" with her.

No way in hell I owed Ameline anything.

After a short honeymoon, Sunny and Frank went back to Austria and began to clean their own house. Naturally, I was right about Celeste. She'd managed to vanish, Sunny pursuing her through her blood tie to the family. Didn't matter. I had no doubt I'd be seeing Celeste again.

For about as long as it took to kill her.

I was surprised to find Demetrius had also gone his own way. I didn't try to find him. I had to remember to ask Gram how she knew him and why I had the feeling there was much more to his story than I first thought.

The small metal box of powder I'd retrieved from the

back of my closet at the castle went into my underwear drawer with my crystal. For safekeeping.

Who knew when I might need it.

My vampire core eventually stopped clinging and went back to her quiet nature, but never again did she hide and stay silent. In fact, I often found myself waking to deep debates between my magicks, as they watched over me, using philosophy and history to pass the time.

Felt like living inside a very small dorm room with too many roommates sometimes. But I was happy to share all the same.

My crystal was thrilled with its new flavor of power, the clan's touch still inside. I made it a point to keep that fact from Sunny, though I felt certain she wouldn't care.

Okay, was pretty sure.

Sashenka had brought up joining the family again before she left after the wedding and though I really liked the idea of her as my second, knew she was a great choice, I still hesitated about talking to Tallah. After all these years, family was the most important thing to me and I didn't know if I was ready to break up hers, happily and with support and best wishes or not.

Because putting them through the opposite was unthinkable.

Now, more than ever, I knew I needed someone beside me I could trust, someone who would stand by me, protect my family, be there unquestioning and always have my back no matter what. As much as I loved my grandmother, I knew she was right. It was time for her to step down and for me to take over.

I'd never risk her again, and there was a whole lot of risk coming.

PATTI LARSEN

Like what you read? Find out more at
pattilarsen.com

Here's a look at the first chapter of
Book Thirteen of the Hayle Coven Novels

DARK PROMISE

Chapter One

I sucked at packing.

Didn't matter how much time I had to do the job, my clothes always ended up scrunched and squished and wrinkled. If I stogged in one more sweater I'd end up never wearing anyway the zipper would bust. And I still had a week before I had to leave for Harvard.

Restless, I went through my closet again, just in case I forgot something important. The sound of laughter from the living room downstairs drifted up and through my open bedroom door, enticing, but not enough to keep my slightly fractured attention. I could have gone down and sat with Gram and Meira, sprawled for Sass to sit on my stomach, privately giggled at how stiff and formal Charlotte held herself even when relaxing in front of a movie, but I just couldn't seem to make myself hold still.

The nightmares and sleeplessness weren't helping. I

felt as though something lived under my skin, crawling around at the least opportune moments, giving me nuclear goosebumps at the mere thought of fangs and blood and lying, dying, under cold stars... I shook myself and went deeper, digging through clothes I forgot I had that would probably fit Meira more than me.

Funny, this was the first time we'd stayed put for as long as I could remember. No more moving suddenly in the middle of the night, forced to wipe memories and run for the hills because someone in the coven let magic slip. Nope, I was tied to this house and to Wilding Springs for the rest of my life—or until the Wild Hunt woke from their slumber in my back yard to destroy the world. Which, thanks to my immortality, would all happen at about the same time.

Sigh. No thinking. Just digging. I giggled over a pair of pale blue sparkly leggings with fur on the bottoms and tossed them over my shoulder. But even the unusual finds of my walk-in weren't enough to keep my attention for long. I finally shut the door and sank to the corner of my bed, shoulders slumped, heart beating a little faster than I liked.

—clammy lips on my neck, the sharp jab of fangs, everything going dark—

My entire body jerked as I sat up straight, both hands pressed to my chest as I forced myself to breathe slowly. Batsheva had almost defeated me, would have killed me if not for my slow evolution to maji. Now that Sunny was ensconced as the Queen of the Wilhelm clan, Uncle Frank beside her as her Prince, the squabbles of the vampires were over. Or, most of them, I hoped. And it brought me great comfort knowing the shell of Batsheva Moromond was in my basement, probably gathering mold. Still alive. Suffering.

Fantabulous.

Still.

I stood and paced toward my dresser, hands shoved in my pockets. This inability to relax was getting on my nerves. All I needed was one good night's sleep. Could it be I was so hooked in to trouble that when things calmed down I couldn't handle it? I hugged myself, forcing my butt into my desk chair, wiggling my mouse to lose myself in the Internet for a little while.

No thinking.

Social media held no attraction, everyone too damned cheery. My emails had been piling up, though, so I took some time to delete the countless offers for gambling, Viagra and finding true love in a foreign country while writing back to my friends who took the time to check in on me.

Tippy's lurid tales of her summer fun made me laugh out loud. Better. Leave it to the sultry red-head Sashenka introduced me to last year to distract me. I answered her with the suggestion she take up writing romance novels before moving on to one from Quaid.

Syd,

Sorry I couldn't be at the wedding, would have liked to be there. Had a chance to go on an assignment and took it. I hope you understand. See you at school.

Love, Q

Understand? My temper sizzled through my demon's magic and almost fried my keyboard. Yeah, I understood. The Enforcers and his life came before family. There was a time when our feelings on such matters were different, when all he craved was family and I wanted out of mine. And while he claimed the Enforcers were his family now, I wasn't buying it.

Nothing mattered as much as the people I loved.

And what was this love business? I calmed down, drawing deep breaths, sitting back before my angry fingers could type a very pissed-off reply I'd regret later. I knew he loved me. I loved him too. But there were times it seemed our priorities were just so out of synch we'd never get it right.

Not that being with him long term was an option anyway. Which led my mind to the maji, my immortality, the vampires.

Twitch. No. Thinking.

I filed his email away for a bit, not ready to answer it in any manner that wouldn't start a fight I wasn't really interesting in having. Instead, I clicked on the next in line, eyes flickering over the smiley face that was the subject heading while my whole body went tense.

Sydlynn,

You still owe me for saving your life.

Oh. My. Swearword. Ameline.

Everything inside me screamed denial, from my demon's roar to Shaylee's shriek, to my vampire's rumbling anger. Even the family magic bubbled and swirled in answer. No. Way. I didn't owe her anything. I didn't ask her to help me when Batsheva and her clan drained me dry, stealing the essence of my vampire from me. I was doing just fine on my own.

Yeah. Just fine. Right, Syd. As much as it hurt, ached, burned, part of me knew Ameline was right.

Damn her. Damn her.

My eyes kept reading while my brain spun in furious circles.

Despite the fact I'd rather take the debt directly from you at some point, I've discovered the means to balance the score without your participation. Consider us even.

Best,

Ameline.

Um, what? Cold sweat leaped to the surface of my skin as my heart skipped once, a thudding beat that brought a moment of darkness. The email was time stamped only a half hour ago.

What was she up to? What had she done?

Panic gripped me even as I felt a surge of demon magic coming from below me.

Dad. I ran down out my door, down the stairs, pounding around the corner and to the basement door, while Meira called, "Syd, is that Dad?", her footfalls following me. Sassafras's mind touched mine, but I didn't have time to talk to the silver Persian, to give him anything.

Ameline couldn't have hurt Dad. He was on Demonicon. This was a coincidence.

Just a coincidence.

I skidded to a halt after almost falling down the last three steps, staring in fear at Dad's diamond effigy. Mom had covered it when Dad was forced to break their mating after being tricked into taking Second Seat. But I'd contacted him since then, refused to cut him out of my life.

He was still my father.

The demon magic hovered, but no Dad. I reached for him, panic dimming a little. This was crazy. Ameline was messing with my head. I was right, just a coincidence after all.

"Syd?" Meira stopped on the bottom step, a frown creasing her forehead as amber fire flamed in her eyes. "Was that Dad?"

I didn't answer, focused on the magic I'd felt, the surge that usually preceded his arrival. But no one called him. Were we imagining things? I reached for it, let my demon sniff around the touch that brought me downstairs.

The moment I contacted the demon magic pooled in the basement, the veil jerked open and powerful amber energy wrapped around me. I heard Meira calling my name, Sassafras, Charlotte's choked cry, even as I hurtled head-first through the tear in the barrier between planes to land painfully on my hands and knees on cold stone. The sizzling crack of the veil sealing behind me was so loud I almost cried out, breathless enough I managed only a whimper.

Thick black nails with red-tinted skin supported me as I pushed myself up and looked around. The large room was dark and chill, outlines of black furnishings familiar, as were the two large windows I faced.

Ahbi's room. My grandmother. What was I doing here and who brought me?

My eyes scanned as I rose to my feet, feeling my demon surge inside, my vision improving immediately in the darkened room. Just enough I could make out a shape collapsed on the floor.

"Ahbi!" I was moving before I knew it, stumbling to fall on my abused knees at her side, where my grandmother sprawled, facing away from me. I reached for her, pulling her toward me, feeling something hot and slick on my skin. Jerked away on impulse, stomach knotted at the scent of copper now very familiar to me.

Looked down.

Choked on a sob of disbelief.

My hands were covered in blood.

About the Author

Everything you need to know about me is in this one statement: I've wanted to be a writer since I was a little girl, and now I'm doing it. How cool is that, being able to follow your dream and make it reality? I've tried everything from university to college, graduating the second with a journalism diploma (I sucked at telling real stories), am part of an all-girl improv troupe (if you've never tried it, I highly recommend making things up as you go along as often as possible). I've even been in a Celtic girl band (some of our stuff is on YouTube!) and was an independent film maker. My life has been one creative thing after another—all leading me here, to writing books for a living.

PATTI LARSEN

Now with multiple series in happy publication, I live on beautiful and magical Prince Edward Island (I know you've heard of Anne of Green Gables) with my very patient husband and multitude of pets.

I love-love-love hearing from you! You can reach me (and I promise I'll message back) at patti@pattilarsen.com. And if you're eager for your next dose of Patti Larsen books (usually about one release a month) come join my mailing list! All the best up and coming, giveaways, contests and, of course, my observations on the world (aren't you just dying to know what I think about everything?) all in one place: http://smarturl.it/PattiLarsenEmail.

Last—but not least!—I hope you enjoyed what you read! Your happiness is my happiness. And I'd love to hear just what you thought. A review where you found this book would mean the world to me—reviews feed writers more than you will ever know. So, loved it (or not so much), **your honest review would make my day**. Thank you!

www.ingramcontent.com/pod-product-compliance
Lightning Source LLC
LaVergne TN
LVHW051111080426
835510LV00018B/1995